COCHRANE

2013

D0357006

HAUNTED
TRAIL
TALES

HAUNTED TRAIL TALES

Paranormal Stories from the Woods

Edited by Amy Kelley Hoitsma

GUILFORD, CONNECTICUT
HELENA, MONTANA

AN IMPRINT OF GLOBE PEQUOT PRESS

To buy books in quantity for corporate use
or incentives, call **(800) 962-0973**
or e-mail **premiums@GlobePequot.com**.

FALCON GUIDES®

Copyright © 2012 Morris Book Publishing, LLC

ALL RIGHTS RESERVED. No part of this book may be reproduced or transmitted in any form by any means, electronic or mechanical, including photocopying and recording, or by any information storage and retrieval system, except as may be expressly permitted in writing from the publisher. Requests for permission should be addressed to Globe Pequot Press, Attn: Rights and Permissions Department, PO Box 480, Guilford, CT 06437.

FalconGuides is an imprint of Globe Pequot Press.

Falcon, FalconGuides, and Outfit Your Mind are registered trademarks of Morris Book Publishing, LLC.

Grateful acknowledgment is made to those who granted permission to reprint the selections in this book. A complete list of copyright permissions is on page 125.

Library of Congress Cataloging-in-Publication Data is available on file.

ISBN 978-0-7627-8125-6

Printed in the United States of America

10 9 8 7 6 5 4 3 2 1

CONTENTS

INTRODUCTION

You don't believe in ghosts? Then I dare you to take this book along on your next camping trip.

Imagine: You're camping out in the deep, dark woods. You've finished dinner and are huddled around a blazing campfire. Someone pulls out the book and starts reading one of the stories out loud.

You feel the hair start to stand straight up on the back of your neck. You hear some unrecognizable sound, at first far away . . . then closer . . . and closer. You *swear* you saw something move out of the corner of your eye, but when you turn to look—*nothing*.

Your sixth sense—the one that feels the presence of things unseen—is working overtime. You feel as thought you're being watched. Your everyday "reality" suddenly feels far, far away. You start to think that the idea of spirits, angels, and ghosts isn't unbelievable at all!

In this collection of stories about ghosts and their encounters with the living, it's up to you to decide whether they're true. Is it possible that a dead woman actually phoned her husband to tell him they would meet soon in the afterworld? Did the ghost of a murdered man's dog really kill his assassin? And what about the guy who was literally scared to death in that dark old mansion?

Or maybe your job is only to listen and let the story take on a life of its own. Or, better yet, to read aloud and make the story come alive with your best scary voice and dramatic pauses.

But I need to warn you: You will be inviting those ghosts to join you. By the time the campfire dies down and you're ready to crawl into your sleeping bag, I suggest you pull the covers of your everyday "reality" back over your head if you want to get some sleep.

I double dog dare you.

Amy Kelley Hoitsma
March 2012

ON THE BRIGHTON ROAD

Richard Barham Middleton

Slowly the sun had climbed up the hard white downs, till it broke with little of the mysterious ritual of dawn upon a sparkling world of snow. There had been a hard frost during the night, and the birds, which hopped about here and there with scant tolerance of life, left no trace of their passage on the silver pavements. In places the sheltered caverns of the hedges broke the monotony of the whiteness that had fallen upon the coloured earth, and overhead the sky melted from orange to deep blue, from deep blue to a blue so pale that it suggested a thin paper screen rather than illimitable space. Across the level fields there came a cold, silent wind that blew a fine dust of snow from the trees but hardly stirred the crested hedges. Once above the skyline, the sun seemed to climb more quickly, and as it rose higher it began to give out a heat that blended with the keenness of the wind.

It may have been this strange alternation of heat and cold that disturbed the tramp in his dreams, for he struggled for a moment with the snow that covered him, like a man who finds himself twisted uncomfortably in the bedclothes, and then sat up with staring, questioning eyes. "Lord! I thought I was in bed," he said to himself as he took in the vacant landscape, "'and all the while I was out here." He stretched his limbs, and, rising carefully to his feet, shook the snow off his body. As he did so the wind set him shivering, and he knew that his bed had been warm.

"Come, I feel pretty fit," he thought. "I suppose I am lucky to wake at all in this. Or unlucky—it isn't much of a business to come back to." He looked up and saw the downs shining against the blue like the Alps on a picture-postcard. "That means another forty miles or so, I suppose," he continued grimly. "Lord knows what I did yesterday. Walked till I was done, and now I'm only about twelve miles from Brighton. Damn the snow, damn Brighton, damn everything!" The sun crept higher and higher, and he started walking patiently along the road with his back turned to the hills.

"Am I glad or sorry that it was only sleep that took me, glad or sorry, glad or sorry?" His thoughts seemed to arrange themselves in a metrical accompaniment to the steady thud of his footsteps, and he hardly sought an answer to his question. It was good enough to walk to.

Presently, when three milestones had loitered past, he overtook a boy who was stooping to light a cigarette. He wore no overcoat and looked unspeakably fragile against the snow. "Are you on the road, guv'nor?" asked the boy huskily as he passed.

"I think I am," the tramp said.

"Oh! Then I'll come a bit of the way with you if you don't walk too fast. It's a bit lonesome walking this time of day." The tramp nodded his head, and the boy started limping along by his side.

"I'm eighteen," he said casually. "I bet you thought I was younger."

"Fifteen, I'd have said."

"You'd have backed a loser. Eighteen last August, and I've been on the road six years. I ran away from home five times when I was a little 'un, and the police took me back each time. Very good to me, the police was. Now I haven't got a home to run away from."

"Nor have I," the tramp said calmly.

"Oh, I can see what you are," the boy panted; "you're a gentleman come down. It's harder for you than for me." The tramp glanced at the limping, feeble figure and lessened his pace.

"I haven't been at it as long as you have," he admitted.

"No, I could tell that by the way you walk. You haven't got tired yet. Perhaps you expect something at the other end?"

The tramp reflected for a moment. "I don't know," he said bitterly; "I'm always expecting things."

"You'll grow out of that," the boy commented. "It's warmer in London, but it's harder to come by grub. There isn't much in it really."

"Still, there's the chance of meeting somebody there who will understand—"

"Country people are better," the boy interrupted. "Last night I took a lease of a barn for nothing and slept with the cows, and this morning the farmer routed me out and gave me tea and toke because I was so little. Of course I score there; but in London, soup on the Embankment at night, and all the rest of the time coppers moving you on."

"I dropped by the roadside last night and slept where I fell. It's a wonder I didn't die," the tramp said. The boy looked at him sharply.

"How do you know you didn't?" he said. "I don't see it," the tramp said, after a pause.

"I tell you," the boy said hoarsely, "people like us can't get away from this sort of thing if we want to. Always hungry and thirsty and dog-tired and walking all the time. And yet if anyone offers me a nice home and work, my stomach feels sick. Do I look strong? I know I'm little for my age, but I've been knocking about like this for six years, and do you think I'm not dead? I was drowned bathing at Margate, and I was killed by a gypsy with a spike; he knocked my head right in. And twice I was froze like you last night, and a motor cut me down on this very road, and yet I'm walking along here now, walking to London to walk away from it again, because I can't help it. Dead! I tell you we can't get away if we want to."

The boy broke off in a fit of coughing, and the tramp paused while he recovered.

"You'd better borrow my coat for a bit, Tommy," he said, "your cough's pretty bad."

"You go to hell!" the boy said fiercely, puffing at his cigarette; "I'm all right. I was telling you about the road. You haven't got down to it yet, but you'll find out presently. We're all dead, all of us who're on it; and we're all tired, yet somehow we can't leave it. There's nice smells in the summer, dust and hay and the wind smack in your face on a hot day; and it's nice waking up in the wet grass on a fine morning. I don't know, I don't know—" he lurched forward suddenly, and the tramp caught him in his arms.

"I'm sick," the boy whispered—"sick."

The tramp looked up and down the road, but he could see no houses or any sign of help. Yet even as he supported the boy doubtfully in the middle of the road a motorcar suddenly flashed in the middle distance and came smoothly through the snow.

"What's the trouble?" said the driver quietly as he pulled up. "I'm a doctor." He looked at the boy keenly and listened to his strained breathing.

"Pneumonia," he commented. "I'll give him a lift to the infirmary, and you, too, if you like."

The tramp thought of the workhouse and shook his head. "I'd rather walk," he said.

The boy winked faintly as they lifted him into the car. "I'll meet you beyond Reigate," he murmured to the tramp. "You'll see." And the car vanished along the white road.

All the morning the tramp splashed through the thawing snow, but at midday he begged some bread at a cottage door and crept into a lonely barn to eat it. It was warm in there, and after his meal he fell asleep among the hay. It was dark when he woke and started trudging once more through the slushy roads.

Two miles beyond Reigate a figure, a fragile figure, slipped out of the darkness to meet him.

"On the road, guv'nor?" said a husky voice. "Then I'll come a bit of the way with you if you don't walk too fast. It's a bit lonesome walking this time of day."

"But the pneumonia!" cried the tramp, aghast.

"I died at Crawley this morning," said the boy.

THE GIRL AND THE GHOST

Laura Simms

On an island in the Northwest there lived a chief who had three beautiful daughters. "This is my true wealth," he boasted. He became very rich from the marriages of his two elder girls and said to his wife, "Our youngest daughter is more lovely than the older ones. She could fetch an even greater bride price." Young men traveled from far and wide to seek her hand, but the chief turned them away, saying, "Their offerings are too small."

The village was remote and had enjoyed years of peace and prosperity. No one lacked fish or seal, and the people were protected by ancient myth and custom. Their homes sat safely between earth and sky and sea. They had had no complaint with the chief, but now the old people warned him, "Your desire is unnatural. It will bring only disaster and unhappiness." He mocked them for their belief in old tales, saying, "You spend too much time listening to ghost stories and gossip. Times have changed."

One night the chief and his wife were awakened by the sound of singing. The most enchanting voices filled the night air. By the time they were dressed and standing outside, finely carved canoes had pulled to their shore.

A noble young man stood before all the other strangers. He wore a blanket adorned with turquoise, feathers, and beads. His black hair shone like silk. Behind him were painted boxes, piles of blankets, copper trinkets, feathered capes, baskets, silver, bowls, and skins.

The stranger approached, offering an elegant greeting to the chief, his wife, and the daughter. Then he asked for the young woman's hand in marriage. She watched, impressed by his dignity and language. The chief, seeing the abundance of gifts, agreed to the wedding.

"I am honored," said the stranger. "And I ask that the wedding be held tonight, since I must return to my own people before dawn."

The chief had the people awakened, although it was the middle of the night, and the bonfires were lit. Food was cooked.

Dances and songs were performed, and gifts were exchanged. And before sunrise the handsome bridegroom sat with his new bride by his side in the largest canoe and rowed away from the island.

Everyone in the village was entranced by the beautiful singing and stood on the shore until the wedding party had vanished in the distance. Only then did the chief's wife say, as if arising from a dream, "We never asked the name of the land where our daughter is going."

"Do not worry," the chief assured her. "They will return when their first child is born, as is the custom." The chief was satisfied with his newfound wealth and slept deeply.

Meanwhile the young bride sat beside her new husband. She was filled with joy, imagining the life they would lead together. Her husband and his people were friendly, and their songs were more wonderful than any she had heard in her village.

Then in the shadowy mist of the first light of dawn, she saw an island appear, like the back of a seal rising out of the water. The voices that greeted them were joyful. Young women her own age helped her onto the land and led her to her house. A hundred people made a path for them to walk through. She saw children in circles playing games and old people laughing and gossiping in the distance.

When she yawned her husband took her hand and whispered, "We can sleep all day, and in the evening I will tell you all you need to know about this land."

The house she entered was new. She smelled sweet cedar and noticed beautiful baskets and shiny pots. The blanket on their bed was red and yellow and blue. The two lay down to rest beneath it, and no sooner did she put her head on his shoulder than she drifted into sleep. He caressed her hair and said, "It has been a long journey."

She wasn't accustomed to sleeping during the day, and when the sun was bright, she opened her eyes. It was unearthly quiet. Startled, she sat up. Light streamed through broken walls. The pots were tarnished, and a musty smell filled the air. The baskets she had admired had unraveled, and the blanket was faded. Only then did she realize that the body lying next to her was icy cold. Turning, she stared into the empty sockets of a skull.

She tried to scream, but no sound issued forth. As she moved away from the skull, it fell to the side with a click. Frantic, she threw open the door to seek help.

She saw only white sand and yellowing bones. Skeletons everywhere. No flesh, no faces—only bones. She stepped over the dead carefully and raced to the shore. Leaping over the corpses lying there, she took hold of a canoe and shoved it into the water. But it moved through her fingers like a feather, dissolving like moth-eaten cloth.

"There must be a living person on this land somewhere," she assured herself. "Surely there must be someone in this place." Scanning the shore, she saw nothing. Then in the distance she made out a house with smoke rising.

She stepped cautiously among the skeletons and walked toward the house. Yet the farther she walked, the more distant it seemed. At first she was careful of the bones, but when fear gripped her again, she grew careless, stepping on the bodies, kicking the bones to the left and the right. The cracking bones pierced the silence like the cry of a gull.

By late afternoon she stood before a house. Its small door opened, but no one greeted her. Slowly she went in. In the dim light she saw an ancient woman as small as a child, sitting in the middle of the room, weaving blankets with her own hair. Her eyes were large, and her face was lined with wrinkles.

The girl sobbed, but the woman said, "My name is Screech Owl Woman. I will not harm you. You must be the one our chief married in the night."

"I want to go home," the girl stuttered.

"Why are you awake in the daylight?" asked the Old One, putting down her weaving.

"Please," the girl begged, "Let me go home."

Screech Owl Woman motioned her closer. "They should have told you where you are. This is the land of the dead, and your husband is the chief of ghosts."

The young woman closed her eyes and moaned, "I am not dead."

"You can't go home now," the old woman said softly. "When you learn about the land of the dead, you will not be unhappy. Sit beside me, and I will tell you all you need to know about the laws of this land. Here things are reversed from the ways of the world of the living. But this land is not evil. The ghosts are charming, and your husband is the most kind of all."

The girl sat down, and Screech Owl Woman described the land of the dead and the rules that bound the ghosts to that world. Slowly the young woman from the land of the living grew less afraid.

As time passed, it began to grow dark. She heard voices, beautiful voices singing, and she knew that the ghosts were taking back their skins. At first the voices sounded friendly. But as they grew louder, a chill ran up her spine. "They are coming for me," she gasped.

The footsteps of the ghosts racing on the sand pounded like a hundred drums. They were calling for Screech Owl Woman to give them the girl.

"She has killed many ghosts!" shouted one. "Many have lost their arms or their legs," complained another.

A third wailed, "Her husband's head has been twisted to one side."

The Old One went to the door. The girl begged her not to give her back to them. But she blinked and nodded for the girl to follow.

At the sight of Screech Owl Woman, the ghosts grew still. "It is your fault," she reprimanded the ghosts, as if they were her children. "You should have told her where she was. Have no anger. I have instructed her, and now she can return peacefully to her husband.

"I am always here," Screech Owl Woman said to the girl. Reluctantly the wife of the chief returned with the ghosts.

The house was as it had been the night before. Everything was new. Her husband lay beneath the many-colored blanket and wore a bandage around his neck. He smiled, and she placed her cool hand on his forehead to comfort him. Gladly, then, she sat beside him.

It wasn't long before she grew accustomed to sleeping during the day and being awake at night. She learned to live among the ghosts and grew to love her husband.

Everything was fine until she gave birth to a baby. The ghosts didn't like her son. "He is neither child nor ghost," they complained. At last the chief of the ghosts decided to take her back to her homeland.

One night he laid his son on a wooden board and covered him with twelve cloths. "Take the boy to the land of your parents," he said sadly. "He will live the life of a human child, and in time he will know death, but I will not know him again. You must promise that no one will look upon his face for twelve days and twelve nights. Then he will be a child. If he is seen, I will return for you, and he will be a ghost forever."

The princess embraced her husband and promised to follow his instructions. Then she took the strange bundle in her arms, and that night they paddled back to this world.

In the land of the living the moon was full. The chief and his wife awoke again to the sound of singing and remarked, "They have returned." The chief's wife could not hide her joy and said, "She holds a baby."

But upon the couple's arrival the girl stepped solemnly out of the canoe, and the husband turned and left without saying a word.

"Mother, Father," the girl said slowly, "you married me to the chief of the ghosts, and I have lived in the land of the dead."

That night she explained why they could not see their grandchild for twelve days and twelve nights. They stayed awake until dawn, and she described the world of the ghosts and how they lived during the night.

She was glad to be home, and the days passed quickly. Once again she became accustomed to sleeping in the nighttime and being awake during the day. She rarely went outside. Mainly she sat with the baby on her knees and rocked him, singing songs from both worlds.

But as the days passed, she grew lonely for company. Finally, on the morning of the twelfth day, she asked her mother to watch the child while she visited with a friend. "In a few hours we can see his face. Then my son will be like other children," she said, and she departed cheerfully.

The grandmother took the baby on her knees as her daughter had done day after day and rocked him back and forth, singing songs that had been sung to her as a child and songs she had sung to her daughters.

Then she said to herself, "How strange this is. No one has ever seen the face of a ghost, and I am holding a ghost from the land of the dead. What a pity that we will never know how they look." The baby cooed and giggled, and the grandmother held him closer. "In just a few hours he will be like every other child." Then she said, "What harm would it be if I just looked quickly? Then we would know how they appear. No one need fear. I will barely look at his face."

As quiet as a cloud, she shut the door and took off the first cloth. The baby moved. "Hush, little prince," she whispered, and she took off the second cloth. She removed the third and fourth. The baby grew still. She lifted the fifth and the sixth. "You are quiet, my little one," she hummed. She removed the seventh and eighth and ninth cloths. The bundle grew lighter. Then she took off the tenth, and a chill breeze swept under the door into the room. With hands trembling, she took off the eleventh cloth. "One more, my little man," she said, and she slowly grasped the edge of the cloth and removed it from his face.

Screaming, she dropped the bundle to the floor. A tiny skeleton shattered, bits of it flying in every direction, and worms and maggots crawled between the bones.

At that very instant the girl fell ill. She left the house of her friend and ran to her mother's lodge. She opened the door, then fell to the floor and began to gather up the bones of her baby. Weeping, she placed them on the board in the shape of the boy and gently touched each one. Then she covered him again with the cloths. "Mother, why did you look?" she said, with pity but no anger, and taking the baby, she left the house.

As the sun went down, she heard her husband singing. Her father and mother stood by their house in silence, side by side, and watched as she returned to the land of the dead.

That night her son became a ghost, and she in time became a ghost as well. She returned to the land of the living only one more time, but she never touched the earth.

When the boy was three years old, on the night of a full moon, she rowed out to sea, singing. She held the child up in the moonlight for the chief and his wife to see.

Since that time no one has traveled from the land of the dead to the land of the living. And no one has gone from this world to that. No one, that is, except old Screech Owl Woman, who still travels back and forth but is never seen in her human form. You can still hear her eerie song at night, and sometimes you can see her shadow in the moonlight.

BLIND MAN'S BUFF

H. Russell Wakefield

"Well, thank heavens that yokel seemed to know the place," said Mr. Cort to himself. "'First to the right, second to the left, black gates.' I hope the oaf in Wendover who sent me six miles out of my way will freeze to death. It's not often like this in England—cold as the penny in a dead man's eye." He'd barely reach the place before dusk. He let the car out over the rasping, frozen roads. "First to the right" must be this; "second to the left" must be this—and there were the black gates. He got out, swung them open, and drove cautiously up a narrow, twisting drive, his headlights peering suspiciously round the bends. Those hedges wanted clipping, he thought, and this lane would have to be remetalled—full of holes. Nasty drive up on a bad night; would cost some money, though.

The car began to climb steeply and swing to the right, and presently the high hedges ended abruptly and Mr. Cort pulled up in front of Lorn Manor. He got out of the car, rubbed his hands, stamped his feet, and looked about him.

Lorn Manor was embedded halfway up a Chiltern spur and, as the agent had observed, "commanded extensive vistas." The place looked its age, Mr. Cort decided, or rather ages, for the double Georgian brick chimneys warred with the Queen Anne left front. He could just make out the date, 1703, at the base of the nearest chimney. All that wing must have been added later. "Big place, marvellous bargain at seven thousand; can't understand it. How those windows with their little curved eyebrows seem to frown down on one!" And then he turned and examined the "vistas." The trees were tinted exquisitely to an uncertain glory as the great red sinking sun flashed its rays on their crystal mantle. The Vale of Aylesbury was drowsing beneath a slowly deepening shroud of mist. Above it the hills, their crests rounded and shaded by silver and rose coppices, seemed to have set in them great smoky eyes of flame where the last rays burned in them.

"It is like some dream world," thought Mr. Cort. "It is curious how wherever the sun strikes it seems to make an eye, and each one fixed on me; those hills, even those windows. But judging from that mist, I shall have a slow journey home; I'd better have a quick look inside, though I have already taken a prejudice against the place—I hardly know why. Too lonely and isolated, perhaps." And then the eyes blinked and closed, and it was dark. He took a key from his pocket and went up three steps and thrust it into the keyhole of the massive oak door. The next moment he looked forward into absolute blackness, and the door swung to and closed behind him. This, of course, must be the "palatial panelled hall" that the agent described. He must strike a match and find the light switch. He fumbled in his pockets without success, and then he went through them again. He thought for a moment. "I must have left them on the seat in the car," he decided; "I'll go and fetch them. The door must be just behind me here."

He turned and groped his way back, and then drew himself up sharply, for it had seemed that something had slipped past him, and then he put out his hands—to touch the back of a chair, brocaded, he judged. He moved to the left of it and walked into a wall, changed his direction, went back past the chair, and found the wall again. He went back to the chair, sat down, and went through his pockets again, more thoroughly and carefully this time. Well, there was nothing to get fussed about; he was bound to find the door sooner or later. Now, let him think. When he came in he had gone straight forward, three yards perhaps; but he couldn't have gone straight back, because he'd stumbled into this chair. The door must be a little to the left or right of it. He'd try each in turn. He turned to the left first and found himself going down a little narrow passage; he could feel its sides when he stretched out his hands. Well, then, he'd try the right. He did so, and walked into a wall. He groped his way along it, and again it seemed as if something slipped past him. "I wonder if there's a bat in here?" he asked himself, and then found himself back at the chair.

How Rachel would laugh if she could see him now. Surely he had a stray match somewhere. He took off his overcoat and ran his hands round the seam of every pocket, and then he did the same to the coat and waistcoat of his suit. And then he put them on again. Well, he'd try again. He'd follow the wall along. He did so and found himself in a narrow passage. Suddenly he shot out his right hand, for he had the impression that something had brushed his face very lightly. "I'm beginning to get a little bored with that bat, and with this blasted room generally," he said to himself. "I could imagine a more nervous person than myself getting a little fussed and panicky; but that's the one thing not to do." Ah, here was that chair again. "Now I'll try the wall on the other side." Well, that seemed to go on forever, so he retraced his steps till he found the chair, and sat down again. He whistled a little snatch resignedly. What an echo! The little tune had been flung back at him so fiercely, almost menacingly. Menacingly: That was just the feeble, panicky word a nervous person would use. Well, he'd go to the left again this time.

As he got up a quick spurt of cold air fanned his face. "Is anyone there?" he said. He had purposely not raised his voice—there was no need to shout. Of course no one answered. Who could there have been to answer, since the caretaker was away? Now let him think it out. When he came in he must have gone straight forward and then swerved slightly on the way back; therefore—no, he was getting confused. At that moment he heard the whistle of a train and felt reassured. The line from Wendover to Aylesbury ran half-left from the front door, so it should be about there—he pointed with his finger, got up, groped his way forward, and found himself in a little narrow passage. Well, he must turn back and go to the right this time. He did so, and something seemed to slip just past him, and then he scratched his finger slightly on the brocade of the chair. "Talk about a maze," he thought to himself; "it's nothing to this." And then he said to himself, under his breath: "Curse this vile, Godforsaken place!" A silly, panicky thing to do he realized—almost as bad as shouting aloud. Well, it was obviously no use trying to find the door, he *couldn't* find it—*couldn't*. He'd sit in the chair till the light came. He sat down.

How very silent it was; his hands began searching in his pockets once more. Except for that sort of whispering sound over on the left somewhere—except for that, it was absolutely silent—except for that. What could it be? The caretaker was away. He turned his head slightly and listened intently. It was almost as if there were several people whispering together. One got curious sounds in old houses. How absurd it was! The chair couldn't be more than three or four yards from the door. There was no doubt about that. "I must be slightly to one side or the other." He'd try the left once more. He got up, and something lightly brushed his face. "Is anyone there?" he said, and this time he knew he had shouted. "Who touched me? Who's whispering? Where's the door?" What a nervous fool he was to shout like that; yet someone outside might have heard him. He went groping forward again, and touched a wall. He followed along it, touching it with his fingertips, and there was an opening.

The door, the door, it must be! And he found himself going down a little narrow passage. He turned and ran back. And then he remembered! He had put a match-booklet in his notecase! What a fool to have forgotten it, and have made such an exhibition of himself. Yes, there it was; but his hands were trembling, and the booklet slipped through his fingers. He fell to his knees and began searching about on the floor. "It must be just here, it can't be far"— and then something icy-cold and damp was pressed against his forehead. He flung himself forward to seize it, but there was nothing there. And then he leapt to his feet, and with tears streaming down his face cried: "Who is there? Save me! Save me!" And then he began to run round and round, his arms outstretched. At last he stumbled against something, the chair— and something touched him as it slipped past. And then he ran screaming round the room;

and suddenly his screams slashed back at him, for he was in a little narrow passage.

N ow, Mr. Runt," said the coroner, "you say you heard screaming coming from the direction of the Manor. Why didn't you go to find out what was the matter?"

"None of us chaps goes to Manor after sundown," said Mr. Runt.

"Oh, I know there's some absurd superstition about the house; but you haven't answered the question. There were screams, obviously coming from someone who wanted help. Why didn't you go to see what was the matter, instead of running away?"

"None of us chaps goes to Manor after sundown," said Mr. Runt.

"Don't fence with the question. Let me remind you that the doctor said Mr. Cort must have had a seizure of some kind, but that had help been quickly forthcoming, his life might have been saved. Do you mean to tell me that even if you had known this, you would still have acted in so cowardly a way?"

Mr. Runt fixed his eyes on the ground and fingered his cap.

"None of us chaps goes to Manor after sundown," he repeated.

THE CASE OF VINCENT PYRWHIT

Barry Pain

The death of Vincent Pyrwhit, JP, of Ellerdon House, in the county of Buckinghamshire, would in the ordinary way have received no more attention than the death of any other simple country gentleman. The circumstances of his death, however, though now long since forgotten, were sensational and attracted some notice at the time. It was one of those cases that is easily forgotten within a year, except just in the locality where it occurred. The most sensational circumstances of the case never came before the public at all. I give them here simply and plainly. The psychical people may make what they like of them.

Pyrwhit himself was a very ordinary country gentleman, a good fellow, but in no way brilliant. He was devoted to his wife, who was some fifteen years younger than himself and remarkably beautiful. She was quite a good woman, but she had her faults. She was fond of admiration, and she was an abominable flirt. She misled men very cleverly, and was then sincerely angry with them for having been misled. Her husband never troubled his head about these flirtations, being assured quite rightly that she was a good woman. He was not jealous; she, on the other hand, was possessed of a jealousy amounting almost to insanity. This might have caused trouble if he had ever provided her with the slightest basis on which her jealousy could work, but he never did. With the exception of his wife, women bored him. I believe she did once or twice try to make a scene for some preposterous reason that was no reason at all; but nothing serious came of it, and there was never a real quarrel between them.

On the death of his wife after a prolonged illness, Pyrwhit wrote and asked me to come down to Ellerdon for the funeral and to remain at least a few days with him. He would be quite alone, and I was his oldest friend. I hate attending funerals, but I *was* his oldest friend, and I was, moreover, a distant relation of his wife. I had no choice, and I went down.

There were many visitors in the house for the funeral, which took place in the village churchyard, but they left immediately afterwards. The air of heavy gloom that had hung over the house seemed to lift a little. The servants (servants are always emotional) continued to break down at intervals, noticeably Pyrwhit's man, Williams, but Pyrwhit himself was self-possessed. He spoke of his wife with great affection and regret, but still he could speak of her and not unsteadily. At dinner he also spoke of one or two other subjects, of politics and of his duties as a magistrate, and of course he made the requisite fuss about his gratitude to me for coming down to Ellerdon at that time. After dinner we sat in the library, a room well and expensively furnished but without the least attempt at taste. There were a few oil paintings on the walls, a presentation portrait of himself and a landscape or two—all more or less bad, as far as I remember. He had eaten next to nothing at dinner, but he had drunk a good deal; the wine, however, did not seem to have the least effect upon him. I had got the conversation definitely off the subject of his wife when I made a blunder. I noticed an

Erichsen's extension standing on his writing table. I said:

"I didn't know that telephones had penetrated into the villages yet."

"Yes," he said, "I believe they are common enough now. I had that one fitted up during my wife's illness to communicate with her bedroom on the floor above us on the other side of the house."

At that moment the bell of the telephone rang sharply.

We both looked at each other. I said with the stupid affectation of calmness one always puts on when one is a little bit frightened:

"Probably a servant in that room wishes to speak to you."

He got up, walked over to the machine, and swung the green cord toward me. The end of it was loose.

"I had it disconnected this morning," he said; "also the door of that room is locked, and no one can possibly be in it."

He had turned the colour of grey blotting paper; so probably had I.

The bell rang again—a prolonged, rattling ring.

"Are you going to answer it?" I said.

"I am not," he answered firmly.

"Then," I said, "I shall answer it myself. It is some stupid trick, a joke not in the best of taste, for which you will probably have to sack one or other of your domestics."

"My servants," he answered, "would not have done that. Besides, don't you see it is impossible? The instrument is disconnected."

"The bell rang all the same. I shall try it."

I picked up the receiver.

"Are you there?" I called.

The voice that answered me was unmistakably the rather high staccato voice of Mrs. Pyrwhit.

"I want you," it said, "to tell my husband that he will be with me tomorrow."

I still listened. Nothing more was said.

I repeated, "Are you there?" and still there was no answer.

I turned to Pyrwhit.

"There is no one there," I said. "Possibly there is thunder in the air affecting the bell in some mysterious way. There must be some simple explanation, and I'll find it all out tomorrow."

He went to bed early that night. All the following day I was with him. We rode together, and I expected an accident every minute, but none happened. All the evening I expected him to turn suddenly faint and ill, but that also did not happen. When at about ten o'clock he excused himself and said goodnight, I felt distinctly relieved. He went up to his room and rang for Williams.

The rest is, of course, well known. The servant's reason had broken down, possibly the immediate cause being the death of Mrs. Pyrwhit. On entering his master's bedroom, without the least hesitation, he raised a loaded revolver that he carried in his hand and shot Pyrwhit through the heart. I believe the case is mentioned in some of the textbooks on homicidal mania.

THE OPEN WINDOW

Saki

My aunt will be down presently, Mr. Nuttel," said a very self-possessed young lady of fifteen; "in the meantime you must try and put up with me."

Framton Nuttel endeavoured to say the correct something that should duly flatter the niece of the moment without unduly discounting the aunt that was to come. Privately he doubted more than ever whether these formal visits on a succession of total strangers would do much toward helping the nerve cure that he was supposed to be undergoing.

"I know how it will be," his sister had said when he was preparing to migrate to this rural retreat; "you will bury yourself down there and not speak to a living soul, and your nerves will be worse than ever from moping. I shall just give you letters of introduction to all the people I know there. Some of them, as far as I can remember, were quite nice."

Framton wondered whether Mrs. Sappleton, the lady to whom he was presenting one of the letters of introduction, came into the nice division.

"Do you know many of the people round here?" asked the niece when she judged that they had had sufficient silent communion.

"Hardly a soul," said Framton. "My sister was staying here, at the rectory, you know, some four years ago, and she gave me letters of introduction to some of the people here."

He made the last statement in a tone of distinct regret.

"Then you know practically nothing about my aunt?" pursued the self-possessed young lady.

"Only her name and address," admitted the caller. He was wondering whether Mrs. Sappleton was in the married or widowed state. An undefinable something about the room seemed to suggest masculine habitation.

"Her great tragedy happened just three years ago," said the child; "that would be since your sister's time."

"Her tragedy?" asked Framton; somehow in this restful country spot tragedies seemed out of place.

"You may wonder why we keep that window wide open on an October afternoon," said the niece, indicating a large French window that opened onto a lawn.

"It is quite warm for the time of the year," said Framton; "but has that window got anything to do with the tragedy?"

"Out through that window, three years ago to a day, her husband and her two young brothers went off for their day's shooting. They never came back. In crossing the moor to their favourite snipe-shooting ground, they were all three engulfed in a treacherous piece of bog. It had been that dreadful wet summer, you know, and places that were safe in other years gave way suddenly without warning. Their bodies were never recovered. That was the dreadful part of it." Here the child's voice lost its self-possessed note and became falteringly human. "Poor Aunt always thinks that they will come back some day, they and the little brown spaniel that was lost with them, and walk in at that window just as they used to do. That is why the window is kept open every evening till it is quite dusk. Poor dear Aunt, she has often told me how they went out, her husband with his white waterproof coat over his arm and Ronnie, her youngest brother, singing 'Bertie, why do you bound?' as he always did to tease her, because she said it got on her nerves. Do you know, sometimes on still, quiet evenings like this, I almost get a creepy feeling that they will all walk in through that window—"

She broke off with a little shudder. It was a relief to Framton when the aunt bustled into the room with a whirl of apologies for being late in making her appearance.

"I hope Vera has been amusing you," she said.

"She has been very interesting," said Framton.

"I hope you don't mind the open window," said Mrs. Sappleton briskly; "my husband and brothers will be home directly from shooting, and they always come in this way. They've been out for snipe in the marshes today, so they'll make a fine mess over my poor carpets. So like you menfolk, isn't it?"

She rattled on cheerfully about the shooting and the scarcity of birds and the prospects for duck in the winter. To Framton it was all purely horrible. He made a desperate but only partially successful effort to turn the talk to a less ghastly topic; he was conscious that his hostess was giving him only a fragment of her attention, and her eyes were constantly straying past him to the open window and the lawn beyond. It was certainly an unfortunate coincidence that he should have paid his visit on this tragic anniversary.

"The doctors agree in ordering me complete rest, an absence of mental excitement, and avoidance of anything in the nature of violent physical exercise," announced Framton, who laboured under the tolerably widespread delusion that total strangers and chance acquaintances are hungry for the least detail of one's ailments and infirmities, their cause and cure. "On the matter of diet they are not so much in agreement," he continued.

"No?" said Mrs. Sappleton, in a voice that only replaced a yawn at the last moment. Then she suddenly brightened into alert attention—but not to what Framton was saying.

"Here they are at last!" she cried. "Just in time for tea, and don't they look as if they were muddy up to the eyes!"

Framton shivered slightly and turned toward the niece with a look intended to convey sympathetic comprehension. The child was staring out through the open window with dazed horror in her eyes. In a chill shock of nameless fear, Framton swung round in his seat and looked in the same direction.

In the deepening twilight three figures were walking across the lawn toward the window; they all carried guns under their arms, and one of them was additionally burdened with a white coat hung over his shoulders. A tired brown spaniel kept close at their heels. Noiselessly they neared the house, and then a hoarse young voice chanted out of the dusk: "I said, Bertie, why do you bound?"

Framton grabbed wildly at his stick and hat; the hall door, the gravel drive, and the front gate were dimly noted stages in his headlong retreat. A cyclist coming along the road had to run into the hedge to avoid an imminent collision.

"Here we are, my dear," said the bearer of the white mackintosh, coming in through the window; "fairly muddy, but most of it's dry. Who was that who bolted out as we came up?"

"A most extraordinary man, a Mr. Nuttel," said Mrs. Sappleton; "could only talk about his illnesses, and dashed off without a word of good-bye or apology when you arrived. One would think he had seen a ghost."

"I expect it was the spaniel," said the niece calmly; "he told me he had a horror of dogs. He was once hunted into a cemetery somewhere on the banks of the Ganges by a pack of pariah dogs and had to spend the night in a newly dug grave with the creatures snarling and grinning and foaming just above him. Enough to make anyone lose their nerve."

Romance at short notice was her speciality.

STALEY FLEMING'S HALLUCINATION

Ambrose Bierce

Of two men who were talking, one was a physician.

"I sent for you, Doctor," said the other, "but I don't think you can do me any good. Maybe you can recommend a specialist in psychopathy. I fancy I'm a bit loony."

"You look all right," the physician said.

"You shall judge—I have hallucinations. I wake every night and see in my room, intently watching me, a big black Newfoundland dog with a white forefoot."

"You say you wake; are you sure about that? 'Hallucinations' are sometimes only dreams."

"Oh, I wake all right. Sometimes I lie still a long time, looking at the dog as earnestly as the dog looks at me—I always leave the light going. When I can't endure it any longer, I sit up in bed—and nothing is there!

"M, 'm—what is the beast's expression?"

"It seems to me sinister. Of course I know that, except in art, an animal's face in repose has always the same expression. But this is not a real animal. Newfoundland dogs are pretty mild looking, you know; what's the matter with this one?"

"Really, my diagnosis would have no value: I am not going to treat the dog."

The physician laughed at his own pleasantry but narrowly watched his patient from the corner of his eye. Presently he said: "Fleming, your description of the beast fits the dog of the late Atwell Barton."

Fleming half rose from his chair, sat again, and made a visible attempt at indifference. "I remember Barton," he said. "I believe he was—it was reported that—wasn't there something suspicious in his death?"

Looking squarely now into the eyes of his patient, the physician said: "Three years ago the body of your old enemy, Atwell Barton, was found in the woods near his house and yours. He had been stabbed to death. There have been no arrests; there was no clue. Some of us had 'theories.' I had one. Have you?"

"I? Why, bless your soul, what could I know about it? You remember that I left for Europe almost immediately afterward—a considerable time afterward. In the few weeks since my return, you could not expect me to construct a 'theory.' In fact, I have not given the matter a thought. What about his dog?"

"It was first to find the body. It died of starvation on his grave."

We do not know the inexorable law underlying coincidences. Staley Fleming did not, or he would perhaps not have sprung to his feet as the night wind brought in through the open window the long wailing howl of a distant dog. He strode several times across the room in the steadfast gaze of the physician then, abruptly confronting him, almost shouted: "What has all this to do with my trouble, Dr. Halderman? You forget why you were sent for." Rising, the physician laid his hand upon his patient's arm and said, gently: "Pardon me. I cannot diagnose your disorder offhand—tomorrow, perhaps. Please go to bed, leaving your door unlocked; I will pass the night here with your books. Can you call me without rising?"

"Yes, there is an electric bell."

"Good. If anything disturbs you push the button without sitting up. Good night."

Comfortably installed in an armchair, the man of medicine stared into the glowing coals and thought deeply and long but apparently to little purpose, for he frequently rose and, opening a door leading to the staircase, listened intently then resumed his seat. Presently, however, he fell asleep, and when he woke it was past midnight. He stirred the failing fire, lifted a book from the table at his side, and looked at the title. It was Denneker's *Meditations*. He opened it at random and began to read:

> *Forasmuch as it is ordained of God that all flesh hath spirit and thereby taketh on spiritual powers, so, also, the spirit hath powers of the flesh, even when it is gone out of the flesh and liveth as a thing apart, as many a violence performed by wraith and lemure sheweth. And there be who say that man is not single in this, but the beasts have the like evil inducement, and—*

The reading was interrupted by a shaking of the house, as by the fall of a heavy object.

The reader flung down the book, rushed from the room, and mounted the stairs to Fleming's bedchamber. He tried the door, but contrary to his instructions it was locked. He set his shoulder against it with such force that it gave way. On the floor near the disordered bed, in his nightclothes, lay Fleming, gasping away his life.

The physician raised the dying man's head from the floor and observed a wound in the throat. "I should have thought of this," he said, believing it suicide.

When the man was dead, an examination disclosed the unmistakable marks of an animal's fangs deeply sunken into the jugular vein.

But there was no animal.

TOPAZ

Ruskin Bond

It seemed strange to be listening to the strains of "The Blue Danube" while gazing out at the pine-clad slopes of the Himalayas, worlds apart. And yet the music of the waltz seemed singularly appropriate. A light breeze hummed through the pines, and the branches seemed to move in time to the music. The record player was new, but the records were old, picked up in a junk shop behind the Mall.

Below the pines there were oaks, and one oak tree in particular caught my eye. It was the biggest of the lot and stood by itself on a little knoll below the cottage. The breeze was not strong enough to lift its heavy old branches, but *something* was moving, swinging gently from the tree, keeping time to the music of the waltz, dancing . . .

It was someone hanging from the tree.

A rope oscillated in the breeze, the body turned slowly, turned this way and that, and I saw the face of a girl, her hair hanging loose, her eyes sightless, hands and feet limp; just turning, turning, while the waltz played on.

I turned off the player and ran downstairs.

Down the path through the trees, and onto the grassy knoll where the big oak stood.

A long-tailed magpie took fright and flew out from the branches, swooping low across the ravine. In the tree there was no one, nothing. A great branch extended halfway across the knoll, and it was possible for me to reach up and touch it. A girl could not have reached it without climbing the tree.

As I stood there, gazing up into the branches, someone spoke behind me.

"What are you looking at?"

I swung round. A girl stood in the clearing, facing me. A girl of seventeen or eighteen; alive, healthy, with bright eyes and a tantalizing smile. She was lovely to look at. I hadn't seen such a pretty girl in years.

"You startled me," I said. "You came up so unexpectedly."

"Did you see anything—in the tree?" she asked.

"I thought I saw someone from my window. That's why I came down. Did *you* see anything?"

"No." She shook her head, the smile leaving her face for a moment. "I don't see anything. But other people do—sometimes."

"What do they see?"

"My sister."

"Your *sister*?"

"Yes. She hanged herself from this tree. It was many years ago. But sometimes you can see her hanging there."

She spoke matter-of-factly: Whatever had happened seemed very remote to her.

We both moved some distance away from the tree. Above the knoll, on a disused private tennis court (a relic from the hill station's colonial past) was a small stone bench. She sat down on it: and, after a moment's hesitation, I sat down beside her.

"Do you live close by?" I asked.

"Farther up the hill. My father has a small bakery."

She told me her name—Hameeda. She had two younger brothers.

"You must have been quite small when your sister died."

"Yes. But I remember her. She was pretty."

"Like you."

She laughed in disbelief. "Oh, I am nothing to her. You should have seen my sister."

"Why did she kill herself?"

"Because she did not want to live. That's the only reason, no? She was to have been married, but she loved someone else, someone who was not of her own community. It's an old story, and the end is always sad, isn't it?"

"Not always. But what happened to the boy—the one she loved? Did he kill himself too?"

"No, he took a job in some other place. Jobs are not easy to get, are they?"

"I don't know. I've never tried for one."

"Then what do you do?"

"I write stories."

"Do people *buy* stories?"

"Why not? If your father can sell bread, I can sell stories."

"People must have bread. They can live without stories."

"No, Hameeda, you're wrong. People can't live without stories."

Hameeda! I couldn't help loving her. Just loving her. No fierce desire or passion had taken hold of me. It wasn't like that. I was happy just to look at her, watch her while she sat on the grass outside my cottage, her lips stained with the juice of wild bilberries. She chatted away—about her friends, her clothes, her favourite things.

"Won't your parents mind if you come here every day?" I asked.

"I have told them you are teaching me."

"Teaching you what?"

"They did not ask. You can tell me stories."

So I told her stories.

It was midsummer.

The sun glinted on the ring she wore on her third finger: a translucent golden topaz, set in silver.

"That's a pretty ring," I remarked.

"You wear it," she said, impulsively removing it from her hand. "It will give you good thoughts. It will help you to write better stories."

She slipped it onto my little finger.

"I'll wear it for a few days," I said. "Then you must let me give it back to you."

On a day that promised rain, I took the path down to the stream at the bottom of the hill. There I found Hameeda gathering ferns from the shady places along the rocky ledges above the water.

"What will you do with them?" I asked.

"This is a special kind of fern. You can cook it as a vegetable."

"It is tasty?"

"No, but it is good for rheumatism."

"Do you suffer from rheumatism?"

"Of course not. They are for my grand-mother; she is very old."

"There are more ferns farther upstream," I said. "But we'll have to get into the water."

We removed our shoes and began paddling upstream. The ravine became shadier and nar-rower, until the sun was almost completely shut out. The ferns grew right down to the water's edge. We bent to pick them but instead found ourselves in each other's arms; and sank slowly, as in a dream, into the soft bed of ferns, while overhead a whistling thrush burst out in dark, sweet song.

"It isn't time that's passing by," it seemed to say. "It is you and I. It is you and I . . ."

I waited for her the following day, but she did not come.

Several days passed without my seeing her.

Was she sick? Had she been kept at home? Had she been sent away? I did not even know where she lived, so I could not ask. And if I had been able to ask, what would I have said?

Then one day I saw a boy delivering bread and pastries at the little tea shop about a mile down the road. From the upward slant of his eyes, I caught a slight resemblance to Hameeda. As he left the shop, I followed him up the hill. When I came abreast of him, I asked: "Do you have your own bakery?"

He nodded cheerfully, "Yes. Do you want anything—bread, biscuits, cakes? I can bring them to your house."

"Of course. But don't you have a sister? A girl called Hameeda?"

His expression changed. He was no longer friendly. He looked puzzled and slightly apprehensive.

"Why do you want to know?"

"I haven't seen her for some time."

"We have not seen her either."

"Do you mean she has gone away?"

"Didn't you know? You must have been away a long time. It is many years since she died. She killed herself. You did not hear about it?"

"But wasn't that her sister—your other sister?"

"I had only one sister—Hameeda—and she died when I was very young. It's an old story; ask someone else about it."

He turned away and quickened his pace,

and I was left standing in the middle of the road, my head full of questions that couldn't be answered.

That night there was a thunderstorm. My bedroom window kept banging in the wind. I got up to close it, and, as I looked out, there was a flash of lightning and I saw that frail body again, swinging from the oak tree.

I tried to make out the features, but the head hung down and the hair was blowing in the wind.

Was it all a dream?

It was impossible to say. But the topaz on my hand glowed softly in the darkness. And a whisper from the forest seemed to say, "It isn't time that's passing by, my friend. It is you and I . . ."

A STORY OF DON JUAN

V. S. Pritchett

It is said that on one night of his life Don Juan slept alone, though I think the point has been disputed. Returning to Seville in the spring he was held up, some hours' ride from the city, by the floods of the Quadalquiver, a river as dirty as an old lion after the rains, and was obliged to stay at the *finca* of the Quintero family. The doorway, the walls, the windows of the house, were hung with the black and violet draperies of mourning when he arrived there. God rest her soul (the peasants said), the lady of the house was dead. She had been dead a year. The young Quintero was a widower. Nevertheless Quintero took him in and even smiled to see a gallant spattered and drooping in the rain like a sodden cockerel. There was malice in that smile, for Quintero was mad with loneliness and grief; the man who had possessed and discarded all women was received by a man demented because he had lost only one.

"My house is yours," said Quintero, speaking the formula. There was bewilderment in his eyes; those who grieve do not find the world and its people either real or believable. Irony inflects the voices of mourners, and there was malice, too, in Quintero's further greetings; for grief appears to put one at an advantage, the advantage (in Quintero's case) being the macabre one that he could receive Juan now without that fear, that terror which Juan brought to the husbands of Seville. It was perfect, Quintero thought, that for once in his life Juan should have arrived at an empty house.

There was not even (as Juan quickly ascertained) a maid, for Quintero was served only by a manservant, being unable any longer to bear the sight of women. This servant dried Don Juan's clothes and in an hour or two brought in a bad dinner, food that stamped úp and down in the stomach like people waiting for a coach in the cold. Quintero was torturing his body as well as his mind, and as the familiar pains arrived they agonized him and set him off about his wife. Grief had also made Quintero an actor. His eyes had that hollow, taper-haunted dusk of the theatre as he spoke of the beautiful girl. He dwelled upon their courtship, on details of her beauty and temperament, and how he had rushed her from the church to the marriage bed like a man racing a tray of diamonds through the streets into the safety of a bank vault. The presence of Don Juan turned every man into an artist when he was telling his own love story—one had to tantalize and surpass the great seducer—and Quintero, rolling it all off in the grand manner, could not resist telling that his bride had died on her marriage night.

"Man!" cried Don Juan. He started straight off on stories of his own. But Quintero hardly listened; he had returned to the state of exhaustion and emptiness that is natural to grief. As Juan talked, the madman followed his own thoughts like an actor preparing and mumbling the next entrance, and the thought he had had when Juan had first appeared at his door returned to him: that Juan must be a monster to make a man feel triumphant that his own wife was dead. Half listening, and indigestion aiding, Quintero felt within himself the total hatred of all the husbands of Seville for this diabolical man. And as Quintero brooded upon this, it occurred to him that it was probably not a chance that he had it in his power to effect the most curious revenge on behalf of the husbands of Seville.

The decision was made. The wine being finished, Quintero called for his manservant and gave orders to change Don Juan's room.

"For," said Quintero drily, "his Excellency's visit is an honour, and I cannot allow one who has slept in the most delicately scented room in Spain to pass the night in a chamber that stinks to heaven of goat."

"The closed room?" said the manservant, astonished that the room that still held the great dynastic marriage bed, and which had not been used more than half a dozen times by his master since the lady's death—and then only at the full moon when his frenzy was worst—was to be given to a stranger.

Yet to this room Quintero led his guest and there parted from him with eyes so sparkling with ill intention that Juan, who was sensitive to this kind of point, understood perfectly that the cat was being let into the cage only because the bird had long ago flown out. The humiliation was unpleasant. Juan saw the night stretching before him like a desert.

What a bed to lie in: so wide, so unutterably vacant, so malignantly inopportune! Juan took off his clothes, snuffed the lamp wick. He lay down, conscious that on either side of him lay wastes of sheet, draughty and uninhabited except by the nomadic bug. A desert. To move an arm one inch to the side, to push out a leg, however cautiously, was to enter desolation. For miles and miles the foot might probe, the fingers or the knee explore a friendless Antarctica. Yet to lie rigid and still was to have a foretaste of the grave. And here, too, he was frustrated: For though the wine kept him yawning, that awful food romped in his stomach, jolting him back from the edge of sleep the moment he got there.

There is an art in sleeping alone in a double bed, but naturally this art was unknown to Juan; he had to learn it. The difficulty is easily solved. If you cannot sleep on one side of the bed, you move over and try the other. Two hours or more must have passed before this occurred to Juan. Sullen-headed he advanced into the desert, and the night air lying chill between the sheers flapped, and made him shiver. He stretched out his arm and crawled toward the opposite pillow. Mother of God, the coldness, the more than virgin frigidity of linen! Juan put down his head and, drawing up his knees, he shivered. Soon, he supposed, he would be warm again, but in the meantime ice could not have been colder. It was unbelievable.

Ice was the word for that pillow and those sheets. Ice. Was he ill? Had the rain chilled him that his teeth must chatter like this and his legs tremble? Far from getting warmer he found the cold growing. Now it was on his forehead and his cheeks, like arms of ice on his body, like legs of ice upon his legs. Suddenly in superstition he got up on his hands and stared down at the pillow in the darkness, threw back the bedclothes and looked down upon the sheet; his breath was hot, yet blowing against his cheeks was a breath colder than the grave; his shoulders and body were hot, yet limbs of snow were drawing him down; and just as he would have shouted his appalled suspicion, lips like wet ice unfolded upon his own and he sank down to a kiss, unmistakably a kiss, which froze him like a winter.

In his own room Quintero lay listening. His mad eyes were exalted and his ears were waiting. He was waiting for the scream of horror. He knew the apparition. There would be a scream, a tumble, hands fighting for the light, fists knocking at the door. And Quintero had locked the door. But when no scream came, Quintero lay talking to himself, remembering the night the apparition had first come to him and had made him speechless and left him choked and stiff. It would be even better if there were no scream!

Quintero lay awake through the night, building castle after castle of triumphant revenge and receiving, as he did so, the ovations of the husbands of Seville. "The stallion is gelded!" At an early hour Quintero unlocked the door and waited downstairs impatiently. He was a wreck after a night like that.

Juan came down at last. He was (Quintero observed) pale. Or was he pale?

"Did you sleep well?" Quintero asked furtively.

"Very well," Juan replied.

"I do not sleep well in strange beds myself," Quintero insinuated. Juan smiled and replied that he was more used to strange beds than his own. Quintero scowled.

"I reproach myself: The bed was large," he said. But the large, Juan said, were necessarily as familiar to him as the strange. Quintero bit his nails. Some noise had been heard in the night—something like a scream, a disturbance. The manservant had noticed it also. Juan answered him that disturbances in the night had indeed bothered him at the beginning of his career, but now he took them in his stride. Quintero dug his nails into the palms of his hands. He brought out the trump.

"I am afraid," Quintero said, "it was a cold bed. You must have *frozen*."

"I am never cold for long," Juan said and, unconsciously anticipating the manner of a poem that was to be written in his memory two centuries later, declaimed: "The blood of Don Juan is hot, for the sun is the blood of Don Juan."

Quintero watched. His eyes jumped like flies to every movement of his guest. He watched him drink his coffee. He watched him tighten the stirrups of his horse. He watched Juan vault into the saddle. Don Juan was humming and when he went off was singing, was singing in that intolerable tenor of his, which was like a cock crow in the olive groves. Quintero went into the house and rubbed his unshaven chin. Then he went out again to the road where the figure of Don Juan was now only a small smoke of dust between the eucalyptus trees. Quintero went up to the room where Juan had slept and stared at it with accusations and suspicions. He called the manservant.

"I shall sleep here tonight," Quintero said.

The manservant answered carefully. Quintero was mad again, and the moon was still only in its first quarter. The man watched his master during the day looking toward Seville. It was too warm after the rains; the country steamed like a laundry.

And then, when the night came, Quintero laughed at his doubts. He went up to the room, and as he undressed he thought of the assurance of those ice-cold lips, those icicle fingers, and those icy arms. She had not come last night; oh what fidelity! To think, he would say in his remorse to the ghost, that malice had so disordered him that he had been base and credulous to use the dead for a trick.

Tears were in his eyes as he lay down, and for some time he dared not turn on his side and stretch out his hand to touch what, in his disorder, he had been willing to betray. He loathed his heart. He craved—yet how could he hope for it now?—the miracle of recognition and forgiveness. It was this craving that moved him at last. His hands went out. And they were met.

The hands, the arms, the lips moved out of their invisibility and soundlessness toward him. They touched him, they clasped him, they drew him down, but—what was this? He gave a shout, he fought to get away, kicked out and swore; and so the manservant found him wrestling with the sheets, striking out with fists and knees, roaring that he was in hell. Those hands, those lips, those limbs, he screamed, were *burning* him. They were of ice no more. They were of fire.

THE TOWER

Marghanita Laski

The road begins to rise in a series of gentle curves, passing through pleasing groves of olives and vines. Five kilometres on the left is the fork for Florence. To the right may be seen the Tower of Sacrifice (470 steps), built in 1535 by Niccolo di Ferramano; superstitious fear left the tower intact when, in 1549, the surrounding village was completely destroyed...

Triumphantly Caroline lifted her finger from the fine italic type. There was nothing to mar the success of this afternoon. Not only had she taken the car out alone for the first time, driving unerringly on the right-hand side of the road, but what she had achieved was not a simple drive but a cultural excursion. She had taken the Italian guidebook Neville was always urging on her, and hesitantly, haltingly, she had managed to piece out enough of the language to choose a route that took in four well-thought-of frescoes, two universally admired campaniles, and one wooden crucifix in a village church quite a long way from the main road. It was not, after all, such a bad thing that a British Council meeting had kept Neville in Florence. True, he was certain to know all about the campaniles and the frescoes, but there was just a chance that he hadn't discovered the crucifix, and how gratifying if she could, at last, have something of her own to contribute to his constantly accumulating hoard of culture.

But could she add still more? There was at least another hour of daylight, and it wouldn't take more than thirty-five minutes to get back to the flat in Florence. Perhaps there would just be time to add this tower to her dutiful collection? What was it called? She bent to the guidebook again, carefully tracing the text with her finger to be sure she was translating it correctly, word by word.

But this time her moving finger stopped abruptly at the name of Niccolo di Ferramano. There had risen in her mind a picture—no, not a picture, a portrait—of a thin white face with deep-set black eyes that stared intently into hers. *Why a portrait?* she asked, and then she remembered.

It had been about three months ago, just after they were married, when Neville had first brought her to Florence. He himself had already lived there for two years and during that time had been at least as concerned to accumulate Tuscan culture for himself as to disseminate English culture to the Italians. What more natural than that he should wish to share—perhaps even to show off—his discoveries to his young wife?

Caroline had come out to Italy with the idea that when she had worked through one or two galleries and made a few trips—say to Assisi and Sienna—she would have done her duty as a British Council wife and could then settle down to examining the Florentine shops, which everyone had told her were too marvellous for words. But Neville had been contemptuous of her programme. "You can see the stuff in the galleries at any time," he had said, "but I'd like you to start with the pieces that the ordinary tourist doesn't see," and of course Caroline couldn't possibly let herself be classed as an ordinary tourist. She had been proud to accompany Neville to castles and palaces privately owned to which his work gave him entry, and there to gaze with what she hoped was pleasure on the undiscovered Raphael, the Titian that had hung on the same wall ever since it was painted, the Giotto fresco under which the family that had originally commissioned it still said their prayers.

It had been on one of these pilgrimages that she had seen the face of the young man with the black eyes. They had made a long slow drive over narrow ill-made roads and at last had come to a castle on the top of a hill. The family was, to Neville's disappointment, away, but the housekeeper remembered him and led them to a long gallery lined with five centuries of family portraits.

Though she could not have admitted it even to herself, Caroline had become almost anaesthetized to Italian art. Dutifully she had followed Neville along the gallery, listening politely while in his light well-bred voice he had told her intimate anecdotes of history, and involuntarily she had let her eyes wander round the room, glancing anywhere but at the particular portrait of Neville's immediate dissertation.

It was thus that her eye was caught by a face on the other side of the room, and forgetting what was due to politeness, she caught her husband's arm and demanded, "Neville, who's that girl over there?"

But he was pleased with her. He said, "Ah, I'm glad you picked that one out. It's generally thought to be the best thing in the collection—a Bronzino of course," and they went over to look at it.

The picture was painted in rich pale colours, a green curtain, a blue dress, a young face with calm brown eyes under plaits of honey-gold hair. Caroline read out the name under the picture—*Giovanna di Ferramano, 1531–1549*. That was the year the village was destroyed, she remembered now, sitting in the car by the roadside, but then she had exclaimed, "Neville, she was only eighteen when she died."

"They married young in those days," Neville commented, and Caroline said in surprise, "Oh, she was married?" It had been the radiantly virginal character of the face that had caught at her inattention.

"Yes, she was married," Neville answered and added, "Look at the portrait beside her. It's Bronzino again. What do you think of it?"

And this was when Caroline had seen the pale young man. There were no clear, light colours in this picture. There was only the whiteness of the face, the blackness of the eyes, the hair, the clothes, and the glint of gold letters on the pile of books on which the young man rested his hand. Underneath this picture was written *Portrait of an Unknown Gentleman*.

"Do you mean he's her husband?" Caroline asked. "Surely they'd know if he was, instead of calling him an Unknown Gentleman?"

"He's Niccolo di Ferramano all right," said Neville. "I've seen another portrait of him somewhere, and it's not a face one would forget, but," he added reluctantly, because he hated to admit ignorance, "there's apparently some queer scandal about him, and though they don't turn his picture out, they won't even mention his name. Last time I was here, the old Count himself took me through the gallery. I asked him about little Giovanna and her husband." He laughed uneasily. "Mind you, my Italian was far from perfect at that time, but it was horribly clear that I shouldn't have asked." "But what did he *say*?" Caroline demanded. "I've tried to remember," said Neville. "For some reason it stuck in my mind. He said either 'She was lost' or 'She was damned,' but which word it was I can never be sure. The portrait of Niccolo he just ignored altogether."

"What was wrong with Niccolo, I wonder?" mused Caroline, and Neville answered, "I don't know, but I can guess. Do you notice the lettering on those books up there, under his hand? It's all in Hebrew or Arabic. Undoubtedly the unmentionable Niccolo dabbled in Black Magic."

Caroline shivered. "I don't like him," she said. "Let's look at Giovanna again," and they had moved back to the first portrait, and Neville had said casually, "Do you know, she's rather like you."

"I've just got time to look at the tower," Caroline now said aloud, and she put the guidebook back in the pigeonhole under the dashboard and drove carefully along the gentle curves until she came to the fork for Florence on the left.

On the top of the little hill to the right stood a tall round tower. There was no other building in sight. In a land where every available piece of ground is cultivated, there was no cultivated ground around this tower. On the left was the fork for Florence: on the right a rough track led up to the top of the hill.

Caroline knew that she wanted to take the fork to the left, to Florence and home and Neville and—said an urgent voice inside her—for safety. This voice so much shocked her that she got out of the car and began to trudge up the dusty track toward the tower.

After all, I may not come this way again, she argued; it seems silly to miss the chance of seeing it when I've already got a reason for being interested. I'm only just going to have a quick look—and she glanced at the setting sun, telling herself that she would indeed have to be quick if she were to get back to Florence before dark.

And now she had climbed the hill and was standing in front of the tower. It was built of narrow red bricks, and only thin slits pierced its surface right up to the top where Caroline could see some kind of narrow platform encircling it. Before her was an arched doorway. I'm just going to have a quick look, she assured herself again, and then she walked in.

She was in an empty room with a low arched ceiling. A narrow stone staircase clung to the wall and circled round the room to disappear through a hole in the ceiling.

"There ought to be a wonderful view at the top," said Caroline firmly to herself, and she laid her hand on the rusty rail and started to climb, and as she climbed, she counted.

"—thirty-nine, forty, forty-one," she said, and with the forty-first step she came through the ceiling and saw over her head, far far above, the deep blue evening sky, a small circle of blue framed in a narrowing shaft round which the narrow staircase spiralled. There was no inner wall; only the rusty railing protected the climber on the inside.

"—eighty-three, eighty-four—" counted Caroline. The sky above her was losing its colour and she wondered why the narrow slit windows in the wall had all been so placed that they spiralled round the staircase too high for anyone climbing it to see through them.

"It's getting dark very quickly," said Caroline at the hundred-and-fiftieth step. "I know what the tower is like now. It would be much more sensible to give up and go home."

At the two-hundred-and-sixty-ninth step, her hand, moving forward on the railing, met only empty space. For an interminable second she shivered, pressing back to the hard brick on the other side. Then hesitantly she groped forward, upward, and at last her fingers met the rusty rail again, and again she climbed.

But now the breaks in the rail became more and more frequent. Sometimes she had to climb several steps with her left shoulder pressed tightly to the brick wall before her searching hand could find the tenuous rusty comfort again.

At the three-hundred-and-seventy-fifth step, the rail, as her moving hand clutched it, crumpled away under her fingers. "I'd better just go by the wall," she told herself, and now her left hand traced the rough brick as she climbed up and up.

"Four-hundred-and-twenty-two, four-hundred-and-twenty-three," counted Caroline with part of her brain. "I really ought to go down now," said another part. "I wish—oh, I want to go down now—" but she could not. "It would be so silly to give up," she told herself, desperately trying to rationalize what drove her on. "Just because one's afraid—" and then she had to stifle that thought too, and there was nothing left in her brain but the steadily mounting tally of the steps.

"—four-hundred-and-seventy!" said Caroline aloud with explosive relief, and then she stopped abruptly because the steps had stopped too. There was nothing ahead but a piece of broken railing barring her way, and the sky, drained now of all its colour, was still some twenty feet above her head.

"But how idiotic," she said to the air. "The whole thing's absolutely pointless," and then the fingers of her left hand, exploring the wall beside her, met not brick but wood.

She turned to see what it was, and there in the wall, level with the top step, was a small wooden door. "So it does go somewhere after all," she said, and she fumbled with the rusty handle. The door pushed open and she stepped through.

She was on a narrow stone platform about a yard wide. It seemed to encircle the tower.

The platform sloped downward away from the tower, and its stones were smooth and very shiny—and this was all she noticed before she looked beyond the stones and down.

She was immeasurably, unbelievably high and alone and the ground below was a world away. It was not credible, not possible that she should be so far from the ground. All her being was suddenly absorbed in the single impulse to hurl herself from the sloping platform. "I cannot go down any other way," she said, and then she heard what she said and stepped back, frenziedly clutching the soft rotten wood of the doorway with hands sodden with sweat. There is no other way, said the voice in her brain, there is no other way.

"This is vertigo," said Caroline. "I've only got to close my eyes and keep still for a minute and it will pass off. It's bound to pass off. I've never had it before, but I know what it is and it's vertigo." She closed her eyes and kept very still and felt the cold sweat running down her body.

"I should be all right now," she said at last, and carefully she stepped back through the doorway onto the four-hundred-and-seventieth step and pulled the door shut before her. She looked up at the sky, swiftly darkening with night. Then, for the first time, she looked down into the shaft of the tower, down to the narrow unprotected staircase spiralling round and round and round, and disappearing into the dark. She said—she screamed—"I can't go down."

She stood still on the top step, staring downward, and slowly the last light faded from the tower. She could not move. It was not possible that she should dare to go down, step by step down the unprotected stairs into the dark below. It would be much easier to fall, said the voice in her head, to take one step to the left and fall and it would all be over. You cannot climb down.

She began to cry, shuddering with the pain of her sobs. It could not be true that she had brought herself to this peril, that there could be no safety for her unless she could climb down the menacing stairs. The reality *must* be that she was safe at home with Neville—but this was the reality, and here were the stairs; at last she stopped crying and said, "Now I shall go down."

"One!" she counted and, her right hand tearing at the brick wall, she moved first one and then the other foot down to the second step. "Two!" she counted, and then she thought of the depth below her and stood still, stupefied with terror. The stone beneath her feet, the brick against her hand were too frail protections for her exposed body. They could not save her from the voice that repeated that it would be easier to fall. Abruptly she sat down on the step.

"Two," she counted again, and spreading both her hands tightly against the step on each side of her, she swung her body off the second step, down on to the third. "Three," she counted, then "four" then "five," pressing closer and closer into the wall, away from the empty drop on the other side.

At the twenty-first step she said, "I think I can do it now." She slid her right hand up the rough wall and slowly stood upright. Then with the other hand she reached for the railing it was now too dark to see, but it was not there.

For timeless time she stood there, knowing nothing but fear. "Twenty-one," she said, "twenty-one," over and over again, but she could not step on to the twenty-second stair.

Something brushed her face. She knew it was a bat, not a hand, that touched her, but still it was horror beyond conceivable horror, and it was this horror, without any sense of moving from dread to safety, that at last impelled her down the stairs.

"Twenty-three, twenty-four, twenty-five—" she counted, and around her the air was full of whispering skin-stretched wings. If one of should touch her again, she must fall. "Twenty-six, twenty-seven, twenty-eight—" The skin of her right hand was torn and hot with blood, for she would never lift it from the wall, only press it slowly down and force her rigid legs to move from the knowledge of each step to the peril of the next.

So Caroline came down the dark tower. She could not think. She could know nothing but fear. Only her brain remorselessly recorded the tally. "Five-hundred-and-one," it counted, "five-hundred-and-two—and three—and four—"

A SNAP OF THE FINGERS

Robert D. San Souci

Many years ago Miguel, a boy from the country, visited his grandfather in Mexico City. The old man lived on a pleasant tree-shaded street; but there was one house he shunned. He warned his grandson, "Stay away from that place. The owner, Don Rodrigo, is evil. It is said he serves the devil."

Then Miguel's grandfather explained that Don Rodrigo had been a captain in the Spanish royal army. He had fought so well that the king of Spain had rewarded him by making him a don and giving him official duties in Mexico City.

At first Don Rodrigo had been an honest and respected man of very modest means. Then, one night, a raven had flown to his window during a storm. After this, Don Rodrigo became rich and powerful but corrupt. He never went to church, and he openly made fun of all things holy. This offended his neighbors. Worse yet, he named the raven El Diablo. And it truly was a devil: Miguel's grandfather assured the boy that no one doubted this for a minute.

Don Rodrigo would sit at a window or on one of the several balconies of his house, snapping his fingers. Then the raven would come and perch beside him.

"I have heard from Don Rodrigo's servants," Miguel's grandfather said, "that the bird soils the floors and furnishings, tears the chairs and drapes with its beak, and throws down and shatters the glass and china. But when Don Rodrigo storms at his servants about the damage—and he is a most violent man, Miguel, who uses violent language—the servants just tell him the raven made the mischief. Then Don Rodrigo becomes calm again. 'If it is the work of the devil,' he says, 'then it is well done!' Such a wicked man!" Miguel's grandfather said, "You must stay away from him and that accursed bird."

But Miguel was curious. He would often watch Don Rodrigo in the street. The man lived richly, eating from dishes of solid silver carried by servants wearing clothes embroidered with gold. Yet he dressed like a beggar. Over his shirt and breeches he wore a long cape reaching almost to his heels, which the king of Spain had given him. It bore the emblem of the king himself. When Don Rodrigo wore it, he commanded respect. Yet even this cape, Miguel saw, was shabby and greasy and covered with stains.

The raven, El Diablo, was always preening itself. Its feathers were glossy and unruffled. Secretly Miguel put out corn and bread, and the bird often came to him. It would gobble up the food greedily then watch him. From the way it looked at him—head cocked to one side, eyes staring into his own—Miguel almost felt it was going to speak to him. Then from the nearby house would come the snapping of Don Rodrigo's fingers and the call "El Diablo!" and the bird would fly off.

Two days before Miguel was to return home, Don Rodrigo discovered him feeding the raven in the alley beside his grandfather's house. "Traitor!" the man shrieked at the bird, and he tried to grab it. But the raven gave a mocking cry and flew to safety. Then the man turned on Miguel. "Has the miserable creature struck a bargain with you? *Tell me!*" he yelled.

Confused and frightened, Miguel fled down the alley, while Don Rodrigo shouted threats after him. The boy did not tell his grandfather what had happened. But he swept every trace of corn and breadcrumbs from his windowsill. Then he fastened his shutters.

That night, as he lay in bed, Miguel heard wings beating outside the shutters. Claws slashed at the wood; he heard the *tunk-tunk-tunk* of the raven's razor-sharp beak as it tried to break in. In a panic Miguel took his crucifix off the wall and laid it against the shutters. Instantly the attack stopped. Then the boy heard the faint, impatient snapping of Don Rodrigo's fingers. Then nothing.

The next morning his grandfather's house was abuzz with amazing news. During the night Don Rodrigo's servants had been awakened by terrifying shrieks and pounding from the master's bedroom. When they finally broke down the heavy doors, they found the signs of a terrible struggle: Bedclothes were tossed about, chairs overturned, the doors of the wardrobe were nearly torn off, and most of the clothing inside had been thrown onto the floor. Blood was splashed about, and bloody raven feathers lay in every corner. But there was no other trace of Don Rodrigo or El Diablo.

"Their master, the devil, has carried them off," Miguel's grandfather said. "That is a fitting end to both."

On his last night Miguel slept with his shutters fastened and the cross in place. Once he thought he heard the whirr of wings outside, but he couldn't be sure.

For many reasons, Miguel did not return to Mexico City to visit his grandfather for several years. When he did he found the house of Don Rodrigo empty and falling to ruin. People would cross themselves and hurry past the place.

It was said that the house was haunted. On certain nights, Miguel was told, the ghostly figure of Don Rodrigo could be seen and heard, snapping his fingers and calling, "El Diablo!" Then, with an answering caw, the raven would fly out of the darkness and settle on a windowsill of the dark house, and Don Rodrigo would stroke the bird's back. Then both would vanish.

On Miguel's first night at his grandfather's house, there was a tremendous storm. The lightning and thunder kept him awake. Between thunderclaps Miguel thought he heard a sound like fingers snapping. Opening his window, he became sure that the sound came from Don Rodrigo's house.

As he listened the sound seemed to hypnotize him. He felt he had to obey the summons the way the raven had done. He quickly dressed himself, took a lantern, and followed the sound to Don Rodrigo's house.

The force of the storm had blown the front door open. Like a dreamer, Miguel crossed dusty rooms and climbed the staircase to the second floor. Lightning revealed the open door of a large chamber at the end of the hall. Past a bed, the double doors of a huge wardrobe gaped on the very heart of darkness.

From inside came the snapping, louder than ever. Miguel climbed inside the wardrobe. Something urged him to run his hand over the wooden wall at the back. He discovered a peg that moved, opening the hidden door to a secret room.

In the lamplight Miguel saw the mummified remains of Don Rodrigo; the dust-dry figure was wrapped in the dirty old cape with the king's emblem. But it was spattered with dark blotches. And there were marks upon the face, and wounds still visible on the mummy's chest, that Miguel guessed had been made by the beak and claws of a raven.

Then, to his horror, the right hand snapped its fingers. Half expecting the remains to sit up and speak, Miguel backed away. The next instant the raven flew in and landed on the mummy's wrist. It cocked its head and studied Miguel with glowing eyes.

Too frightened to speak, Miguel just shook his head. The bird's eyes burned into his own. Again he shook his head. With a dart of its beak, the raven snapped off the mummy's thumb and middle finger. Then it flew to Miguel's shoulder and dropped the finger bones into the boy's shirt.

The bones sliding down between his shirt-front and bare chest and the weight of the bird on his shoulder shocked Miguel into action. He swung his lantern around, and the raven hopped back to the mummy with a cry. Miguel, mad with fear for his very soul, threw the lantern at the bird. It flew screeching into the corner as the cape caught fire and the mummy was wrapped in flames.

The raven cried again. Miguel pressed his hands to his ears and fled through the darkened house. The flames followed, setting the place ablaze. Outside, he felt a sudden pinching of the flesh at his stomach—as though some tiny animal were biting him. Horrified he remembered the finger bones still in his shirt. In disgust, he clawed them free and hurled them into one of the urns beside his grandfather's door.

He sealed his shutters with a cross, then prayed until he fell into an exhausted sleep.

The next day he was told that lightning had struck Don Rodrigo's house and burned it to the ground. Miguel tried to convince himself that he had had a dream. But the finger bones at the bottom of the urn told him the truth of what had happened. He buried them in the farthest corner of the garden.

Never again did the ghostly fingers of Don Rodrigo summon the raven. But no matter where he went, Miguel could not put aside the horrors of that night. Worse was the belief that he had only to snap his own fingers and whisper "EI Diablo!" and the bird would come to him. When his life grew difficult, he found it hard to resist the temptation for wealth and power that was only a snap of the fingers away. And this struggle was the worst torture of all.

YUKI-ONNA

Lafcadio Hearn

In a village of Musashi Province, there lived two woodcutters: Mosaku and Minokichi. At the time of which I am speaking, Mosaku was an old man, and Minokichi, his apprentice, was a lad of eighteen years. Every day they went together to a forest situated about five miles from their village. On the way to that forest there is a wide river to cross, and there is a ferryboat. Several times a bridge was built where the ferry is, but the bridge was each time carried away by a flood. No common bridge can resist the current there when the river rises.

Mosaku and Minokichi were on their way home one very cold evening when a great snowstorm overtook them. They reached the ferry, and they found that the boatman had gone away, leaving his boat on the other side of the river. It was no day for swimming, and the woodcutters took shelter in the ferryman's hut—thinking themselves lucky to find any shelter at all. There was no brazier in the hut, nor any place in which to make a fire: It was only a two-mat[1] hut, with a single door but no window. Mosaku and Minokichi fastened the door and lay down to rest, with their straw raincoats over them. At first they did not feel very cold; and they thought that the storm would soon be over.

The old man almost immediately fell asleep; but the boy, Minokichi, lay awake a long time, listening to the awful wind and the continual slashing of the snow against the door. The river was roaring, and the hut swayed and creaked like a junk at sea. It was a terrible storm, and the air was every moment becoming colder, and Minokichi shivered under his raincoat. But at last, in spite of the cold, he too fell asleep.

He was awakened by a showering of snow in his face. The door of the hut had been forced open, and by the snow-light (*yuki-akari*) he saw a woman in the room—a woman all in white. She was bending above Mosaku and blowing her breath upon him—and her breath was

---

1 That is to say, with a floor surface of about six feet square.

like a bright white smoke. Almost in the same moment she turned to Minokichi and stooped over him. He tried to cry out but found that he could not utter any sound. The white woman bent down over him, lower and lower, until her face almost touched him, and he saw that she was very beautiful—though her eyes made him afraid. For a little time she continued to look at him; then she smiled, and she whispered: "I intended to treat you like the other man. But I cannot help feeling some pity for you because you are so young. . . . You are a pretty boy, Minokichi, and I will not hurt you now. But if you ever tell anybody—even your own mother— about what you have seen this night, I shall know it; and then I will kill you. . . . Remember what I say!"

With these words, she turned from him and passed through the doorway. Then he found himself able to move, and he sprang up and looked out. But the woman was nowhere to be seen, and the snow was driving furiously into the hut. Minokichi closed the door and secured it by fixing several billets of wood against it. He wondered if the wind had blown it open; he thought that he might have been only dreaming and might have mistaken the gleam of the snow-light in the doorway for the figure of a white woman. But he could not be sure. He called to Mosaku and was frightened because the old man did not answer. He put out his hand in the dark and touched Mosaku's face, and found that it was ice! Mosaku was stark and dead. . . .

By dawn the storm was over; and when the ferryman returned to his station a little after sunrise, he found Minokichi lying senseless beside the frozen body of Mosaku. Minokichi was promptly cared for and soon came to himself, but he remained a long time ill from the effects of the cold of that terrible night. He had been greatly frightened also by the old man's death; but he said nothing about the vision of the woman in white. As soon as he got well again, he returned to his calling—going alone every morning to the forest and coming back at nightfall with his bundles of wood, which his mother helped him to sell.

One evening in the winter of the following year, as he was on his way home, he overtook a girl who happened to be traveling by the same road. She was a tall, slim girl, very good-looking, and she answered Minokichi's greeting in a voice as pleasant to the ear as the voice of a songbird. Then he walked beside her, and they began to talk. The girl said that her name was

O-Yuki,[2] that she had lately lost both of her parents, and that she was going to Yedo, where she happened to have some poor relations who might help her to find a situation as servant. Minokichi soon felt charmed by this strange girl, and the more that he looked at her, the handsomer she appeared to be. He asked her whether she was yet betrothed, and she answered, laughingly, that she was free. Then, in her turn, she asked Minokichi whether he was married, or pledged to marry; and he told her that, although he had only a widowed mother to support, the question of an "honorable daughter-in-law" had not yet been considered, as he was very young. . . . After these confidences they walked on for a long while without speaking; but, as the proverb declares, *Ki ga aréba, mé mo kuchi hodo ni mono wo iu:* "When the wish is there, the eyes can say as much as the mouth." By the time they reached the village, they had become very much pleased with each other, and then Minokichi asked O-Yuki to rest awhile at his house. After some shy hesitation, she went there with him; and his mother made her welcome and prepared a warm meal for her. O-Yuki behaved so nicely that Minokichi's

---

2 This name, signifying "Snow," is not uncommon.

mother took a sudden fancy to her and per-suaded her to delay her journey to Yedo. And the natural end of the matter was that Yuki never went to Yedo at all. She remained in the house, as an "honorable daughter-in-law."

O-Yuki proved a very good daughter-in-law. When Minokichi's mother came to die—some five years later—her last words were words of affection and praise for the wife of her son. And O-Yuki bore Minokichi ten children, boys and girls—handsome children all of them, and very fair of skin. The country-folk thought O-Yuki a wonderful person, by nature different from themselves. Most of the peasant women age early; but O-Yuki, even after having become the mother of ten children, looked as young and fresh as on the day when she had first come to the village.

One night after the children had gone to sleep, O-Yuki was sewing by the light of a paper lamp. Minokichi, watching her, said:

"To see you sewing there, with the light on your face, makes me think of a strange thing that happened when I was a lad of eighteen. I then saw somebody as beautiful and white as you are now—indeed, she was very like you."

Without lifting her eyes from her work, O-Yuki responded:

"Tell me about her. . . . Where did you see her?"

Then Minokichi told her about the terrible night in the ferryman's hut; and about the White Woman that had stooped above him, smiling and whispering; and about the silent death of old Mosaku. And he said:

"Asleep or awake, that was the only time that I saw a being as beautiful as you. Of course she was not a human being; and I was afraid of her very much afraid—but she was so white! Indeed, I have never been sure whether it was a dream that I saw or the Woman of the Snow."

O-Yuki flung down her sewing and arose and bowed above Minokichi where he sat, and shrieked into his face:

"It was I—I—I! Yuki it was! And I told you then that I would kill you if you ever said one word about it! But for those children asleep there, I would kill you this moment! And now you had better take very, very good care of them; for if ever they have reason to complain of you, I will treat you as you deserve!"

Even as she screamed, her voice became thin, like a crying of wind—then she melted into a bright white mist that spired to the roof beams and shuddered away through the smoke-hole. . . . Never again was she seen.

THE RED ROOM

H. G. Wells

It's your own choosing," said the man with the withered arm once more.

I heard the faint sound of a stick and a shambling step on the flags in the passage outside. The door creaked on its hinges as a second old man entered, more bent, more wrinkled, more aged even than the first. He supported himself by the help of a crutch, his eyes were covered by a shade, and his lower lip, half averted, hung pale and pink from his decaying yellow teeth. He made straight for an armchair on the opposite side of the table, sat down clumsily, and began to cough. The man with the withered hand gave the newcomer a short glance of positive dislike; the old woman took no notice of his arrival, but remained with her eyes fixed steadily on the fire.

"I said—it's your own choosing," said the man with the withered hand, when the coughing had ceased for a while.

"It's my own choosing," I answered.

The man with the shade became aware of my presence for the first time, and threw his head back for a moment, and sidewise, to see me. I caught a momentary glimpse of his eyes, small and bright and inflamed. Then he began to cough and splutter again.

"Why don't you drink?" said the man with the withered arm, pushing the beer toward him. The man with the shade poured out a glassful with a shaking hand, that splashed half as much again on the deal table. A monstrous shadow of him crouched upon the wall, and mocked his action as he poured and drank. I must confess I had scarcely expected these grotesque custodians. There is, to my mind, something inhuman in senility, something crouching and atavistic; the human qualities seem to drop from old people insensibly day by day. The three of them made me feel uncomfortable with their gaunt silences, their bent carriage, their evident unfriendliness to me and to one another. And that night, perhaps, I was in the mood for uncomfortable impressions. I resolved to get away from their vague fore-shadowings of the evil things upstairs.

"If," said I, "you will show me to this haunted room of yours, I will make myself comfortable there."

The old man with the cough jerked his head back so suddenly that it startled me, and shot another glance of his red eyes at me from out of the darkness under the shade, but no one answered me. I waited a minute, glancing from one to the other. The old woman stared like a dead body, glaring into the fire with lack-lustre eyes.

"If," I said, a little louder, "if you will show me to this haunted room of yours, I will relieve you from the task of entertaining me."

"There's a candle on the slab outside the door," said the man with the withered hand, looking at my feet as he addressed me. "But if you go to the Red Room tonight—"

"This night of all nights!" said the old woman, softly.

"—You go alone."

"Very well," I answered, shortly, "and which way do I go?"

"You go along the passage for a bit," said he, nodding his head on his shoulder at the door, "until you come to a spiral staircase; and on the second landing is a door covered with green baize. Go through that, and down the long corridor to the end, and the Red Room is on your left up the steps."

"Have I got that right?" I said, and repeated his directions.

He corrected me in one particular.

"And you are really going?" said the man with the shade, looking at me again for the third time with that queer, unnatural tilting of the face.

"This night of all nights!" whispered the old woman.

"It is what I came for," I said, and moved toward the door. As I did so, the old man with the shade rose and staggered round the table, so as to be closer to the others and to the fire. At the door I turned and looked at them, and saw they were all close together, dark against the firelight, staring at me over their shoulders, with an intent expression on their ancient faces.

"Good-night," I said, setting the door open. "It's your own choosing," said the man with the withered arm.

I left the door wide open until the candle was well alight, and then I shut them in, and walked down the chilly, echoing passage.

I must confess that the oddness of these three old pensioners in whose charge her ladyship had left the castle, and the deep-toned, old-fashioned furniture of the housekeeper's room, in which they foregathered, had affected me curiously in spite of my effort to keep myself at a matter-of-fact phase. They seemed to belong to another age, an older age, an age when things spiritual were indeed to be feared, when common sense was uncommon, an age when omens and witches were credible, and ghosts beyond denying. Their very existence, thought I, is spectral; the cut of their clothing, fashions born in dead brains; the ornaments and conveniences in the room about them even are ghostly—the thoughts of vanished men, which still haunt rather than participate in the world of today. And the passage I was in, long and shadowy, with a film of moisture glistening on the wall, was as gaunt and cold as a thing that is dead and rigid. But with an effort I sent such thoughts to the right-about. The long, drafty subterranean passage was chilly and dusty, and my candle flared and made the shadows cower and quiver. The echoes rang up and down the spiral staircase, and a shadow came sweeping up after me, and another fled before me into the darkness overhead. I came to the wide landing and stopped there for a moment listening to a rustling that I fancied I heard creeping behind me, and then, satisfied of the absolute silence, pushed open the unwilling baize-covered door and stood in the silent corridor.

The effect was scarcely what I expected, for the moonlight, coming in by the great window on the grand staircase, picked out everything in vivid black shadow or reticulated silvery illumination. Everything seemed in its proper position; the house might have been deserted on the yesterday instead of twelve months ago. There were candles in the sockets of the sconces, and whatever dust had gathered on the carpets or upon the polished flooring was distributed so evenly as to be invisible in my candlelight. A waiting stillness was over everything. I was about to advance, and stopped abruptly. A bronze group stood upon the landing hidden from me by a corner of the wall; but its shadow fell with marvelous distinctness upon the white paneling, and gave me the impression of some one crouching to waylay me. The thing jumped upon my attention suddenly. I stood rigid for half a moment, perhaps. Then, with my hand in the pocket that held the revolver, I advanced, only to discover a Ganymede and Eagle, glistening in the moonlight. That incident for a time restored my nerve, and a dim porcelain Chinaman on a buhl table, whose head rocked as I passed, scarcely startled me.

The door of the Red Room and the steps up to it were in a shadowy corner. I moved my candle from side to side in order to see clearly the nature of the recess in which I stood, before opening the door. Here it was, thought I, that my predecessor was found, and the memory of that story gave me a sudden twinge of apprehension. I glanced over my shoulder at the black Ganymede in the moonlight, and opened the door of the Red Room rather hastily, with my face half turned to the pallid silence of the corridor.

I entered, closed the door behind me at once, turned the key I found in the lock within, and stood with the candle held aloft surveying the scene of my vigil, the great Red Room of Lorraine Castle, in which the young Duke had died; or rather in which he had begun his dying, for he had opened the door and fallen headlong down the steps I had just ascended. That had been the end of his vigil, of his gallant attempt to conquer the ghostly tradition of the place, and never, I thought, had apoplexy better served the ends of superstition. There were other and older stories that clung to the room, back to the half-incredible beginning of it all, the tale of a timid wife and the tragic end that came to her husband's jest of frightening her. And looking round that huge shadowy room with its black window bays, its recesses and alcoves, its dusty brown-red hangings and dark gigantic furniture, one could well understand the legends that had sprouted in its black corners, its germinating darknesses. My candle was a little tongue of light in the vastness of the chamber; its rays failed to pierce to the opposite end of the room, and left an ocean of dull red mystery and suggestion, sentinel shadows and watching darknesses beyond its island of light. And the stillness of desolation brooded over it all.

I must confess some impalpable quality of that ancient room disturbed me. I tried to fight the feeling down. I resolved to make a systematic examination of the place, and so, by leaving nothing to the imagination, dispel the fanciful suggestions of the obscurity before they obtained a hold upon me. After satisfying myself of the fastening of the door, I began to walk round the room, peering round each article of furniture, tucking up the valances of the bed and opening its curtains wide. In one place there was a distinct echo to my footsteps, the noises I made seemed so little that they enhanced rather than broke the silence of the place. I pulled up the blinds and examined the fastenings of the several windows. Attracted by the fall of a particle of dust, I leaned forward and looked up the blackness of the wide chimney. Then, trying to preserve my scientific attitude of mind, I walked round and began tapping the oak paneling for any secret opening, but I desisted before reaching the alcove. I saw my face in a mirror—white.

There were two big mirrors in the room, each with a pair of sconces bearing candles, and on the mantelshelf, too, were candles in china candle-sticks. All these I lit one after the other. The fire was laid—an unexpected consideration from the old housekeeper—and I lit it, to keep down any disposition to shiver, and when it was burning well I stood round with my back to it and regarded the room again. I had pulled up a chintz-covered armchair and a table to form a kind of barricade before me. On this lay my revolver, ready to hand. My precise examination had done me a little good, but I still found the remoter darkness of the place and its perfect stillness too stimulating for the imagination. The echoing of the stir and crackling of the fire was no sort of comfort to me. The shadow in the alcove at the end of the room began to display that undefinable quality of a presence, that odd suggestion of a lurking living thing that comes so easily in silence and solitude. And to reassure myself, I walked with a candle into it and satisfied myself that there was nothing tangible there. I stood that candle upon the floor of the alcove and left it in that position.

By this time I was in a state of considerable nervous tension, although to my reason there was no adequate cause for my condition. My mind, however, was perfectly clear. I postulated quite unreservedly that nothing supernatural could happen, and to pass the time I began stringing some rhymes together, Ingoldsby fashion, concerning the original legend of the place. A few I spoke aloud, but the echoes were not pleasant. For the same reason I also abandoned, after a time, a conversation with myself upon the impossibility of ghosts and haunting. My mind reverted to the three old and distorted people downstairs, and I tried to keep it upon that topic.

The sombre reds and grays of the room troubled me; even with its seven candles the place was merely dim. The light in the alcove flaring in a draft, and the fire flickering, kept the shadows and penumbra perpetually shifting and stirring in a noiseless flighty dance. Casting about for a remedy, I recalled the wax candles I had seen in the corridor, and, with a slight effort, carrying a candle and leaving the door open, I walked out into the moonlight, and presently returned with as many as ten. These I put in the various knick-knacks of china with which the room was sparsely adorned, and lit and placed them where the shadows had lain deepest, some on the floor, some in the window recesses, arranging and rearranging them until at last my seventeen candles were so placed that not an inch of the room but had the direct light of at least one of them. It occurred to me that when the ghost came I could warn him not to trip over them. The room was now quite brightly illuminated. There was something very cheering and reassuring in these little silent streaming flames, and to notice their steady diminution of length offered me an occupation and gave me a reassuring sense of the passage of time.

Even with that, however, the brooding expectation of the vigil weighed heavily enough upon me. I stood watching the minute hand of my watch creep towards midnight.

Then something happened in the alcove. I did not see the candle go out, I simply turned and saw that the darkness was there, as one might start and see the unexpected presence of a stranger. The black shadow had sprung back to its place. "By Jove," said I aloud, recovering from my surprise, "that draft's a strong one;" and taking the matchbox from the table, I walked across the room in a leisurely manner to relight the corner again. My first match would not strike, and as I succeeded with the second, something seemed to blink on the wall before me. I turned my head involuntarily and saw that the two candles on the little table by the fireplace were extinguished. I rose at once to my feet.

"Odd," I said. "Did I do that myself in a flash of absent-mindedness?"

I walked back, relit one, and as I did so I saw the candle in the right sconce of one of the mirrors wink and go right out, and almost immediately its companion followed it. The flames vanished as if the wick had been suddenly nipped between a finger and thumb, leaving the wick neither glowing nor smoking, but black. While I stood gaping the candle at the foot of the bed went out, and the shadows seemed to take another step toward me.

"This won't do!" said I, and first one and then another candle on the mantelshelf followed.

"What's up?" I cried, with a queer high note getting into my voice somehow. At that the candle on the corner of the wardrobe went out, and the one I had relit in the alcove followed.

"Steady on!" I said, "those candles are wanted," speaking with a half-hysterical facetiousness, and scratching away at a match the while, "for the mantel candlesticks." My hands trembled so much that twice I missed the rough paper of the matchbox. As the mantel emerged from darkness again, two candles in the remoter end of the room were eclipsed. But with the same match I also relit the larger mirror candles, and those on the floor near the doorway, so that for the moment I seemed to gain on the extinctions. But then in a noiseless volley there vanished four lights at once in different corners of the room, and I struck another match in quivering haste, and stood hesitating whither to take it.

As I stood undecided, an invisible hand seemed to sweep out the two candles on the table. With a cry of terror I dashed at the alcove, then into the corner and then into the window, relighting three as two more vanished by the fireplace, and then, perceiving a better way, I dropped matches on the iron-bound deedbox in the corner, and caught up the bedroom candlestick. With this I avoided the delay of striking matches, but for all that the steady process of extinction went on, and the shadows I feared and fought against returned, and crept in upon me, first a step gained on this side of me, then on that. I was now almost frantic with the horror of the coming darkness, and my self-possession deserted me. I leaped panting from candle to candle in a vain struggle against that remorseless advance.

I bruised myself in the thigh against the table, I sent a chair headlong, I stumbled and fell and whisked the cloth from the table in my fall. My candle rolled away from me and I snatched another as I rose. Abruptly this was blown out as I swung it off the table by the wind of my sudden movement, and immediately the two remaining candles followed. But there was light still in the room, a red light, that streamed across the ceiling and staved off the shadows from me. The fire! Of course I could still thrust my candle between the bars and relight it.

I turned to where the flames were still dancing between the glowing coals and splashing red reflections upon the furniture, made two steps toward the grate, and incontinently the flames dwindled and vanished, the glow vanished, the reflections rushed together and disappeared, and as I thrust the candle between the bars darkness closed upon me like the shutting of an eye, wrapped about me in a stifling embrace, sealed my vision, and crushed the last vestiges of self-possession from my brain. And it was not only palpable darkness, but intolerable terror. The candle fell from my hands. I flung out my arms in a vain effort to thrust that ponderous blackness away from me, and lifting up my voice, screamed with all my might, once, twice, thrice. Then I think I must have staggered to my feet. I know I thought suddenly of the moonlit corridor, and with my head bowed and my arms over my face, made a stumbling run for the door.

But I had forgotten the exact position of the door, and I struck myself heavily against the corner of the bed. I staggered back, turned, and was either struck or struck myself against some other bulky furnishing. I have a vague memory of battering myself thus to and fro in the darkness, of a heavy blow at last upon my forehead, of a horrible sensation of falling that lasted an age, of my last frantic effort to keep my footing, and then I remember no more.

I opened my eyes in daylight. My head was roughly bandaged, and the man with the withered hand was watching my face. I looked about me trying to remember what had happened, and for a space I could not recollect. I rolled my eyes into the corner and saw the old woman, no longer abstracted, no longer terrible, pouring out some drops of medicine from a little blue phial into a glass. "Where am I?" I said. "I seem to remember you, and yet I can not remember who you are."

They told me then, and I heard of the haunted Red Room as one who bears a tale. "We found you at dawn," said he, "and there was blood on your forehead and lips."

I wondered that I had ever disliked him. The three of them in the daylight seemed commonplace old folk enough. The man with the green shade had his head bent as one who sleeps.

It was very slowly I recovered the memory of my experience. "You believe now," said the old man with the withered hand, "that the room is haunted?" He spoke no longer as one who greets an intruder, but as one who condoles with a friend.

"Yes," said I, "the room is haunted."

"And you have seen it. And we who have been here all our lives have never set eyes upon it. Because we have never dared. Tell us, is it truly the old earl who—"

"No," said I, "it is not."

"I told you so," said the old lady, with the glass in her hand. "It is his poor young countess who was frightened—"

"It is not," I said. "There is neither ghost of earl nor ghost of countess in that room; there is no ghost there at all, but worse, far worse, something impalpable—"

"Well?" they said.

"The worst of all the things that haunt poor mortal men," said I; "and that is, in all its nakedness—'Fear!' Fear that will not have light nor sound, that will not bear with reason, that deafens and darkens and overwhelms. It followed me through the corridor, it fought against me in the room—"

I stopped abruptly. There was an interval of silence. My hand went up to my bandages. "The candles went out one after another, and I fled—"

Then the man with the shade lifted his face sideways to see me and spoke.

"That is it," said he. "I knew that was it. A Power of Darkness. To put such a curse upon a home! It lurks there always. You can feel it even in the daytime, even of a bright summer's day, in the hangings, in the curtains, keeping behind you however you face about. In the dusk it creeps in the corridor and follows you, so that you dare not turn. It is even as you say. Fear itself is in that room. Black Fear.... And there it will be... so long as this house of sin endures."

THE STRANGE VALLEY

T. V. Olsen

The three horsemen came up on the brow of a hill, and the valley was below them. It was a broad cup filled by the brooding thickness of the prairie night. The light shed by a narrow sickle of moon picked out just another Dakota valley, about a mile across as the white men reckoned distance, and surrounded by a rim of treeless hills. The valley floor was covered by an ordinary growth of a few small oaks, a lot of brush, and some sandy flats with a sparse lacing of buffalo grass.

Young Elk said, "Is this what you wish us to see, Blue Goose?" He made no effort to keep the skepticism from his voice.

"Yes," said the rider on his left. "This is the place."

"Now that we're here, tell us again what you saw the other night." The third youth, the shaman's son, sounded very intent. "From where did it come?"

"From there." Blue Goose leaned forward as he pointed toward the eastern end of the valley. "As I told you, I'd had a long day of hunting, and I was very tired. I made my camp in the centre of the valley and fell asleep at once. This was about sunset.

"It was long after dark when I woke. I came awake all at once, and I don't know why. I heard a strange sound, a kind of growl that was very low and steady, and it was a long way off. But it was running very fast in my direction, and I sat in my blanket and waited."

Young Elk said with a grim smile, "Because you were too afraid even to run."

Blue Goose was silent for a moment. "Yes," he said honestly. "I was afraid. I didn't know what the thing was, but I knew it was getting closer. And growling louder all the while, as if in great pain or anger. Then I saw it.

"It was a huge beast, as big as a small hill, black in the night and running very close to the ground, and its two eyes were yellow and glaring. It went past me very close, but so fast I didn't think it saw me. It was bellowing as loud as a hundred bull buffaloes if they all bellowed at once. Suddenly it was gone."

"What do you mean, it was gone?" Young Elk demanded. "You said that before."

"I'm not sure. All I know is that suddenly I saw it no more and heard it no more."

"I wish you could tell us more about it," said the shaman's son. "But I suppose it was very dark."

"Yes," Blue Goose agreed. "Even a little darker than tonight." He hesitated. "I thought that the thing might be covered with scales—bright scales like a huge fish—since the moon seemed to glint on it here and there. But I couldn't be sure."

"You're not very sure of anything," Young Elk gibed.

Blue Goose sighed. "I do not know what I saw. As I have said, I left the valley very fast and camped a long way off that night. But I came back in the morning. I looked for the thing's spoor. I looked all over, and there was nothing. Yet I found where I had camped, and my pony's tracks and my own. But the thing left no sign at all."

"Because there had never been a thing. You should be more careful about what you eat, my friend." Young Elk spoke very soberly, though he felt like laughing out loud. "Spoiled meat in one's belly is like *mui waken,* the strong drink. It has a bad effect on the head."

For a little while the three young Sioux sat their ponies in silence, looking down into the dark stillness of the valley. A silky wind pressed up from the valley floor, a wind warm with the summer night and full of the ripening smells of late summer.

But something in it held a faint chill, and that was strange. Young Elk felt a crawl of gooseflesh on his bare shoulders, and he thought: *The night is turning cold, that is all.* He felt the nervous tremor run through his mount.

He laid his hand on the pony's shoulder and spoke quietly to the animal. He was angry at Blue Goose, his best friend, for telling this foolish story and angry at himself for coming along tonight with the other two because he was deeply curious. And back in their camp only a few miles to the north there was firelight and laughter and a warm-eyed girl named Morning Teal, and Young Elk was a fool to be out here with his friend and with the son of that tired old faker of a medicine man.

Of late, Young Elk thought sourly, there had been more than the usual quota of wild stories of visions and bad spirits running rampant among the people. Early this same summer, on the river of the Greasy Grass that the whites called Little Big Horn, the long-haired General Custer had gone down to defeat and death with his troops. Many warriors of their own band had been among the twelve thousand Sioux, Cheyenne, and Arapaho who had helped in the annihilation of a hated enemy.

In the uneasy weeks since, as the people followed the buffalo hunting and drying meat in the prospect of being driven back to the reservation by white cavalry, a rash of weird happenings were reported. Men who had died were seen walking the prairie with bloody arrows protruding from them. Voices of the dead were heard in the night wind. It was the shaman's part to encourage this sort of nonsense. A man claimed that a bluecoat soldier he had scalped appeared to him nightly with the blood still fresh on his head. The shaman chanted gibberish and told him to bury the scalp so that the ghost would trouble his nights no more.

Young Elk was disgusted. He had never seen even one of these spirits. Only the fools who believed in such things ever saw them.

The shaman's son broke the long pause, speaking quietly. "This valley is a strange place. Today I spoke with my father and told him what

Blue Goose has told us. He said that he knows of this place, and that his father's fathers knew of it too. Many strange things happened here in the old days. Men known to be long dead would be seen walking—not as spirits, but in the flesh. Still other things were seen, things too strange to be spoken of. Finally all our people of the Lakotas came to shun the valley. But that was so long ago that even most of the old ones have forgotten the stories."

Young Elk made a rude chuckling sound with his tongue and teeth.

"Young Elk does not believe in such things," the shaman's son observed. "Why then did he come with us tonight?"

"Because otherwise for the next moon I would hear nothing from you and Blue Goose but mad stories about what you saw tonight. I'd prefer to see it for myself."

"Oh," said Blue Goose, "then there *was* something? I did not make this great story out of the air?"

"Maybe not," Young Elk said slyly. "Maybe it was the white man's iron horse that Blue Goose saw."

"Now you jest with me. Even though I am not all-wise like Young Elk, still I know that the iron horse of the *wasicun* runs on two shining rails, and there are no rails here. And the iron horse does not growl thus, nor does it have two eyes that flame in the dark."

Another silence stretched among the three youths as they sat their ponies on the crest of the hill and peered down into the dark valley. And Young Elk thought angrily, *What is this?* They had come here to go down in the valley and wait in the night, in hopes that the thing Blue Goose had seen would make another appearance. Yet they all continued to sit here as though a winter of the spirit had descended and frozen them all to the spot.

Young Elk gave a rough laugh. "Come on!" He kneed his pony forward, down the long grassy dip of hill. The others followed.

Near the bottom, Young Elk's pony turned suddenly skittish, and he had to fight the shying animal to bring him under control. Blue Goose and the shaman's son were having trouble with their mounts too.

"This is a bad omen," panted the shaman's son. "Maybe we had better go back."

"No," Young Elk said angrily, for his pony's behaviour and the strange feeling of the place were putting an edge on his temper. "We've come this far, and now we'll see what there is to see, if anything. Where was Blue Goose when he thought he saw the beast?"

Blue Goose said, "We must go this way," and forced his horse through a heavy tangle of chokecherry brush. He led the way very quickly, as though afraid that his nerve would not hold much longer.

They came to a rather open stretch of sand flats that caught a pale glimmer of moonglow; it was studded with clumps of thicket and a few scrub oaks. "Here is the place," Blue Goose told them.

The three Sioux settled down to wait. Nobody suggested that it would be more comfortable to dismount. Somehow it seemed better to remain on their ponies and accept a cramp or two. It was only, Young Elk told himself, that they should be ready for anything, and they might have a sudden need of the ponies.

Once more it was the shaman's son who ended an interval of silence. "What time of the night did it happen, Blue Goose?"

"I can't be sure. But close to this time, I think."

Silence again. The ponies shuffled nervously. The wind hushed through some dead brush, which rattled like dry, hollow bird bones. Idly Young Elk slipped his throwing-axe from his belt and toyed with it. He slid his hand over the familiar shape of the flint head and the fresh thongs of green rawhide that lashed it to the new handle he had put on only this morning. His palm felt moist.

And his head felt slightly dizzy. Now the shapes of rocks, the black masses of brush, seemed to shimmer and swim; the landscape seemed misty and unreal as if seen through a veil of fog, yet there was no fog. *It is a trick of the moon,* Young Elk thought. He gripped the axe tighter; his knuckles began to ache.

"There!" Blue Goose whispered. "Do you hear it?"

Young Elk snapped, "I hear the wind," but even as the words formed on his lips the sound was increasing, unmistakably not the wind. Not even a gale wind roaring through the treetops of a great forest made such a noise. As yet he could see nothing, but he knew that the sound was moving in their direction.

Suddenly the two yellow eyes of which Blue Goose had spoken came boring out of the night. Now he could see the hulking black shape of the monster running toward them at an incredible speed and so low to the ground that its legs could not be seen. All the while the strange humming roar it made was steadily growing.

The ponies were plunging and rearing with fear. The shaman's son gave a cry of pure panic and achieved enough control over his mount to kick it into a run. In a moment Blue Goose bolted after him.

Young Elk fought his terrified pony down and held the trembling animal steady, his own fear swallowed in an eagerness to have a closer look at the thing. But he was not prepared for the fury of its rush as it bore down toward him. And its round, glaring eyes blinded him—he could see nothing beyond them.

It let out a piercing, horrible shriek as it neared him—it was hardly the length of three ponies away—and it seemed to hesitate. It hissed at him, a long gushing hiss, while the yellow eyes bathed him in their wicked glare.

Young Elk waited no longer. He lunged his pony in an angling run that carried him past the thing's blunt snout, and in that moment brought his arm back and flung the axe with all his strength. He heard it make a strange hollow boom, although he did not see it hit, and then he was racing on through the brush, straining low to his pony's withers, heedless of the tearing branches.

Young Elk did not slow down till he reached the end of the valley; then he looked back without stopping. There was no sign of the beast. The valley was deserted and quiet under the dim moonlight.

Young Elk crossed the rim of hills and caught up with his friends on the prairie beyond. "Did you see it?" the shaman's son demanded eagerly.

"No. Its eyes blinded me. But I hit it with my axe." Young Elk paused; his heart was pounding so fiercely in his chest he was afraid they would hear it, so he went quickly on, "I heard the axe hit the thing. So it was not a ghost."

"How do you know?" countered the shaman's son. "Where did it go? Did you see?"

"No," Young Elk said bitterly. "It was very fast."

"Let's go back to camp," Blue Goose said. "I don't care what the thing was. I do not want to think about it."

J oe Kercheval had been dozing in his seat when his partner, Johnny Antelope, hit the brakes of the big truck and gave Joe a bad jolt. And then Joe nearly blew his stack when Johnny told him the reason he had slammed to an abrupt stop on this long, lonely highway in the middle of nowhere.

"I tell you, I saw him," Johnny insisted as he started up again and drove on. "A real old-time Sioux buck on a spotted pony. He was sitting on his nag right in the middle of the road, and I almost didn't stop in time. Then he came charging past the cab, and I saw him fling something—I think it was an axe—at the truck. I heard it hit. You were waking up just then—you must have heard it."

"I heard a rock thrown up by the wheels hit somewheres against the trailer, that's all," Joe said flatly. "You been on the road too long, kid. You ought to lay off a few weeks, spend a little time with your relatives on the reservation."

Johnny Antelope shook his head. "I saw him, Joe. And then I didn't see him. I mean—I could swear he disappeared—simply vanished into thin air—just as he rode past the cab. Of course it was pretty dark . . ."

"Come off it. For a college-educated Indian, you get some pretty far-out notions. I've made this run a hundred times, and I never seen any wild redskins with axes, spooks or for real."

"You white men don't know it all, Joe. You're Johnny-come-latelies. This has been our country for a long, long time, and I could tell you some things . . ." Johnny paused, squinting through the windshield at the racing ribbon of highway unfolding in the tunnelling brightness of the headlights. "I was just remembering. This is a stretch of land the Sioux have always shunned. There are all kinds of legends concerning it. I remember one story in particular my old grandaddy used to tell us kids—I guess he told it a hundred times or more . . ."

"Nuts on your grandaddy."

Johnny Antelope smiled. "Maybe you're right at that. Old Blue Goose always did have quite an imagination."

"So does his grandson." Joe Kercheval cracked his knuckles. "There's a turnoff just up ahead, kid. Swing around there."

"What for, Joe?"

"We're going back to where you seen that wild man on a horse. I'm gonna prove to you all you seen was moonshine." Joe paused, then added wryly, "Seems like I got to prove it to myself too. I say it was just a rock that hit the truck, and I'll be losin' sleep if I don't find out for sure."

Without another word Johnny swung the big truck round and headed back east on the highway. The two truckers were silent until Johnny slowed and brought the truck to a shrieking stop. The air brakes were still hissing as he leaned from the window, pointing. "Here's the spot, Joe. I recognize that twisted oak on the right."

"OK, let's have a close look." They climbed out of the cab, and Johnny pointed out the exact spot where he had first seen the Indian warrior, and where the warrior had cut off the highway alongside the cab and thrown his axe.

"Look here, kid." Joe played his flashlight beam over the roadside. "Soft shoulders. If your boy left the concrete right here, his horse would of tromped some mighty deep prints in the ground. Not a sign, see?"

"Wait a minute," Johnny Antelope said. "Flash that torch over here, Joe." He stooped and picked up something from the sandy shoulder.

The halo of light touched the thing Johnny held in his outstretched hand. "Know what this is, Joe?" he asked softly. "A Sioux throwing-axe."

Joe swallowed. He started to snort. "Nuts. So it's an axe . . ," but the words died on his lips.

For under the flashlight beam, even as the two men watched, the wooden handle of the axe was dissolving into rotted punk, and the leather fastenings were turning cracked and brittle, crumbling away. Only the stone blade remained in Johnny's hand, as old and flinty and weathered as if it had lain there by the road for an untold number of years . . .

ACKNOWLEDGMENTS

"A Story of Don Juan," copyright 1950, 1983 by V.S. Pritchett, from *More Collected Stories* by V.S. Pritchett. Used by permission of Random House, Inc. Canadian rights: "A Story of Don Juan," reprinted by permission of SLL/Sterling Lord Literistic, Inc. Copyright © by Estate of V. Pritchett.

"A Snap of the Fingers," from *A Terrifying Taste of Short and Shivery: Thirty Creepy Tales* by Robert D. San Souci, copyright © 1998 by Robert D. San Souci. Used by permission of Delacorte Press, an imprint of Random House Children's Books, a division of Random House, Inc.

"Blind Man's Buff," by H. Russell Wakefield. Granted by permission of Academy Chicago Publishers. All rights reserved. Copyright © 1982 by H. Russell Wakefield.

"The Tower" by Marghanita Laski, from *The Third Ghost Book*. Reprinted with permission from David Higham Associates, Ltd.

"The Girl and the Ghost" by Laura Simms, from *Best-Loved Stories Told at the National Storytelling Festival*, © 1991 by the National Association for the Preservation and Perpetuation of Storytelling. Reprinted with permission.

"Topaz" by Ruskin Bond, which appeared in *The Penguin Book of Indian Ghost Stories*, published 1993 by Penguin Books India.

"The Strange Valley," © 1968 T. V. Olsen, which was first published in *Great Ghost Stories of the Old West*, Four Winds Publishing Company, 1968.

ABOUT THE EDITOR

Amy Kelley Hoitsma grew up in a family of five girls in Madison, Wisconsin, where summer days were spent at the neighborhood pool and family vacations were spent camping. Rather than a serene wilderness experience, they were a rowdy family affair, where telling stories around the campfire played an important role.

Today she lives in Bozeman, Montana, with her husband and cat, working primarily as a freelance graphic designer. She gets outside to ski, bike, hike, and camp out at every opportunity.

More books to enjoy around the campfire:

Campfire Stories,
second edition,
by William W. Forgey,
illustrated by Paul G. Hoffman

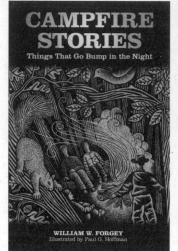

Campfire Tales,
second edition,
by William W. Forgey,
illustrated by Paul G. Hoffman